MY FIFTY YEARS IN Malibu

DOROTHY D. STOTSENBERG

Dorothy D. Stotsenberg
33525 West Mulholland Highway
Malibu, CA 90265
(818) 889-2660
stotsenbe8@aol.com

Published by Pepperdine University Press

Artist credit Yvonne Cherbak

To E. G. S.
Who gave me the best 62 years of my life

ACKNOWLEDGEMENTS

These chapters would never have been collected into book form without the insistence of Paul Almond and Beverly Gosnell. My sincerest thanks to Paul, who became my editor, and to Beverly, who dug up some of the articles I had written more than 30 years ago.

I owe a special debt to Anne Soble, editor of the *Malibu Surfside News* for which I originally wrote many of these stories. Ron Funk, editor of the now defunct *Santa Monica Evening Outlook*, gave me much encouragement in those early days.

Through the years librarians and keepers of archives helped me at the Smithsonian in Washington, D.C. the Huntington Library in Pasadena, the Museum of Natural History in Los Angeles, the Museum of Natural History in Santa Barbara, the Ventura County Historical Society, the Los Angeles County Law Library, the Latter Day Saints Genealogical archives in Westwood Village, and especially Msgr. Francis Weber, of the Mission San Fernando archives.

Even though I had practically stopped swearing at my computer, I needed help, lots of it. Alexander Schulz came to my rescue and put everything in order.

My heartfelt thanks!

TABLE OF CONTENTS

FOREWORD

These chapters are about Malibu through my eyes, a newcomer (in 1949) who later became a seasoned observer. Some stories are from friends who lived through Malibu's "early days." For others I have done extensive research in my career as a journalist to satisfy my curiosity and allow me to portray this fascinating land and its history. I have delved into the Chumash legacy from archaeological reports, many hikes through the area, visits to the Museum of the American Indian Heye Foundation in New York, and in Washington D.C. at the Smithsonian. I have followed the Anza Expeditions day by day as revealed in Herbert Eugene Bolton's graphic translations. I have spent hours in the remarkable San Fernando Mission library with the assistance of Msgr. Francis Weber. I have made my own translation of Don Jose Bartolomeo Tapia's will for the beginnings of Malibu's written history.

The story of Frederick Hastings Rindge and his family has been told and retold, so I decided for the most part not to include it here. It is the theme of the exhibits in the Malibu Lagoon Museum and Adamson Beach House, now a part of the California State Parks System. In part many of these chapters have appeared in the *Malibu Surfside News* and the *Santa Monica Evening Outlook.* Some are a combination of both – brought up-to-date. In Malibu things do not remain the same for very long.

PREFACE

My first view of Malibu was through a wire fence.

The year must have been 1923, the year my family migrated to California from Iowa. The occasion was a Sunday afternoon visit to the "Rindge Castle" then under construction. One of my uncles was a carpenter working on the building. I have no recollection of my father's getting permission to drive through the guarded gates at Las Flores nor of the construction – just of looking through the fence at the expanse of sand.

Some time later, our families, uncle, aunt, cousins, brothers, sister and parents, camped overnight on Topanga Beach. This I remember because the scooped out sand was so uncomfortable for the one night that the next night we children camped out on the floor of our uncle's home. In the morning we experienced our first earthquake, the infamous "Santa Barbara." At the time we kids thought it was funny to watch the chandelier swinging back and forth and to feel the floor rolling under our car seat-cushion beds. In those days we didn't have instant communication, and the next day when we learned about the devastation in Santa Barbara, we didn't think it was so very funny.

Years passed: high school and junior college at Chaffey in Ontario, California; BA at University of Washington in Seattle; first job in Yakima, Washington; marriage; back to Seattle, on to Boston and finally back home to California before Malibu crossed my horizon again.

This time it was for "The Remuda" a very large celebration with lots of horses, a queen, and all kinds of equestrian events, but no lunch. (My husband and I had driven up from Santa Monica "just looking.")

A move to Altadena. After about a year, we realized we had spent every weekend, rain or shine, at the beach. An office dinner brought us to Malibu's famous Sea Lion Café. As we drove along the beach we noticed "For Rent" signs on about half of the little houses bordering the ocean. Most intriguing!

We came back the next Sunday for some "serious looking" and wound up leasing the top floor of an old apartment on Big Rock Beach "for a year to see how we liked it." That was March 1949. (Thirty years later we left the beach for a home in the mountains).

In those days, the inexpensive housing on Big Rock Beach was the "starting point" for young professionals. Our neighbors included an architect, several actors, a doctor, a couple of artists, advertising hopefuls, an aspiring attorney, and some teachers. Over the years we have watched them all achieve success in their fields.

Just before our Big Rock lease was up, luck was with us when the young Texas wife declared "You couldn't pay me to live here!" and we were able to lease Horace Heidt's Carbon Beach house for two years. In 1952, when Mr. Heidt would not renew our lease we walked up the beach, found a house for sale and bought it for $37,500. The same little house in 2001 sold for $3,000,000. We didn't do too badly when in 1978 we sold it for $650,000.

We joined the Malibu Presbyterian Church, the Malibu Riders Club and the Malibu Township Council and soon were in the thick of community activities.

Malibu's origins intrigued me. The year 1950 was just under 100 years since Frederick Hastings Rindge had bought the Rancho Malibu Topango Simi and Sequit and less than 25 years since portions of the Rancho had been subdivided. I became fascinated with stories about how the widowed Mrs. Rindge kept the railroad from laying tracks along the beach, and her unsuccessful efforts to stop the highway from going through her rancho. Thus began my interest in Malibu's historical background.

The articles I have drawn together in this book do not form a consecutive history of Malibu. My editors in both the *Santa Monica Evening Outlook* and the *Malibu Surfside News* gave me "free range" to choose my subjects. Malibu "old-timers" will "remember when," and newcomers will wonder "how come?"

Chapter 1

JOSE BARTOLOMEO TAPIA

Somewhere in my historical readings I came across Herbert Eugene Bolton's graphic translation of the diaries of the second Anza expedition to California. The name "Tapia" fairly jumped off the page. Was this a connection with the Tapia of Malibu, reputedly the first owner of record? It was. I read on.

From the De Anza and Font diaries, I followed the journey through the eyes of the boy, Jose Bartolomeo Tapia. In mission records, I learned about his life as a young soldier, his marriage, and the births of his children. The California Pioneer Registry listed his position in the political life of the Pueblo de Los Angeles. Finally, I procured a copy of his handwritten will. Thus it was easy to imagine a fuller narrative and the beginnings of Malibu as a place in our California history.

Times were hard in the ancient town of Culiacán, Mexico in the 1770s. Two hundred year-old mines were closed. There had been no rain for months and the crops had failed. People existed in miserable poverty.

Don Juan Bautista de Anza, who in 1774 had led an exploratory expedition to Alta California, was commissioned by the King of Spain to lead a second expedition to Monterey and San Francisco to establish a colony there. He reported to Viceroy Bucarelli that he could find good people willing to go as colonists, especially as they would be clothed, fed, and provided with horses and pack mules for the journey, plus payment of one peso a day. Felipe Santiago Tapia, recently widowed father of nine children ranging in age from an infant to a fifteen-year-old daughter, decided to join up. The hero of my story is Tapia's third child and eldest son, Jose Bartolomeo (Bartolo). He was only nine years old when the family - with the addition of a stepmother - set out on the first leg of the journey from Culiacán in May of 1775.

For three whole months the Culiacán band of soldier recruits and families walked a distance of 400 miles to the rendezvous at San Miguel de Horcasitas. They arrived on Friday afternoon, September 29,1775. In another month, the train arrived at Tubac, where the final preparations were made for the long trek north. Here veteran soldiers from Capitan Anza's first expedition to California the previous year joined the group to escort them to San Francisco. The trek began Monday, October 23, 1775.

The veterans and some of their families, the soldier recruits and their families, a few families of civilian colonists, a padre, servants, muleteers, vaqueros and interpreters – the crowd numbered more than two hundred people. With the necessary riding horses, pack mules and cattle, the train stretched for nearly a mile across the desert.

What a life for young Jose Bartolomeo! As their portion of the equipment, the Tapia family had two horses and two mares as well as a pack mule. By the time the family arrived at Tubac, the boy was an accomplished horseman.

As eldest son he was in charge of his eight- and seven-year-old brothers - Juan Jose and Joseph Cristoval - as well as a six-year-old sister, Maria Manuela. Five-year-old Francisco and four-year-old Maria Ygnacia Isadora along with baby Victoriano were in the care of their big sisters, Maria Rosa, and Maria Ana Antonia and the new stepmother, Juana Maria Cardenas. The muleteers tolerated an eager little boy and his friends when they repacked the train early every morning. Jose Bartolomeo surely hung around the presidio veterans to hear their chilling and thrilling stories of Apache raids, especially as the beginning of the trek to California was through Apache country. The Apache had already stolen 500 horses destined for the expedition - causing a month delay.

Young Jose Bartolomeo would have spent time with the Indian, Sebastian Tarabal, the Pima interpreter. He learned catechism from Fr. Fray Pedro Font, the Franciscan priest who accompanied the group and said mass every morning.

When the expedition camped near the Yuma village of Chief Palma on the Colorado River, Jose Bartolomeo would have gone out of his way to make friends with some of the Indian boys his age. He probably caught fish with them in the river for Capitan Anza. Padre Font described them as "bony" - but a fish is a fish.

Along with all of the expedition, Bartolomeo enjoyed his share of the sweet watermelons the Indians gave them - so many they couldn't eat them all, the padre wrote. All agreed that the fresh melons and the vegetables from the Indian gardens were a welcome change from "carne asada" and tortillas, constant fare on the march.

When the going in the desert was hard and there was not enough water for the animals, Capitan Anza put all of the children to work pulling what grass there was and making it into bundles to fit on top of the mules' packs so the riding horses would have something to eat. When streams were dry, they learned about digging "pozos" in the sand and watching the water seep up so the horses and cattle could drink.

How amazed Jose Bartolomeo must have been at his first sight of snow and how he and all the colonists must have suffered from the chill desert winds and cold rain during the months of November and December! The Tapias probably lost one of their horses; so many animals were reported left by the wayside, either dead or dying from weariness, hunger, thirst or the extreme cold. So Bartolo and all of the older children had to walk up and down the hills, scramble over rocks, slog through sand, avoid quicksand and stagger through mud on the way to Mission San Gabriel (in present Pasadena). The group arrived there January 5, 1776, more than seven months after leaving Culiacán.

Capitan Anza, Padre Font and the veteran soldiers immediately rode the 125 miles to San Diego to see what they could do after having heard about an Indian uprising there a short time before. The soldier recruits; the colonists and their families remained at Mission San Gabriel for six weeks, causing a severe shortage of food.

The supply ship was late and with the addition of some 200 more mouths to feed, the mission fathers had to put everyone on half rations.

I can just imagine soldier recruit Felipe Tapia taking his young son over the mountains and out to the ocean to hunt, for this would have been Bartolo's first view of the beautiful land that in later years became his Rancho Topango Malibu.

The expedition finally set out from Mission San Gabriel six weeks later, on February 21,1776. Their second stop, the Padre wrote, was at "Aguas Escondidas" - somewhere along Las Virgenes Creek, just over the hill from Malibu.

Compared to the hardships of the desert winter, travel to Monterey must have seemed easy. The children frolicked on the sandy beaches, explored the tide pools, and clambered over the rocks. On special days the troupe was welcomed with volleys of gunfire and ringing of bells as they reached Missions San Luis Obispo and San Antonio de Los Robles. The songs of the converted Indian neophytes were impressive enough to be remarked in the Padre's diary. The train arrived at Monterey in a rainstorm on Sunday, March 10, 1776.

The Monterey presidio, with the arrival of 100 people (some of the group had remained in San Gabriel) surely was chaos, with horses, cattle, soldiers, women and children all doing their best to find some sort of living quarters amid the spring mud. Families had to pitch their worn tents anywhere they could find a space in the crowded plaza. The horses were confined to a small corral on the point. The Tapia family was crowded in with everyone else, with young Bartolo doing his best to help erect the family's tent. The colonists were ordered to wait in the cramped and crowded Monterey presidio. Capitan Anza and his lieutenant, Don Joseph Juaquin Moraga, set off exploring with a small group of soldiers and Padre Font to select the site for the presidio and the mission - the goal of the expedition. They returned about two weeks later with the news that the place called "San Francisco" was ideal for settlement.

On April 14 Anza and the 10 soldiers from his presidio at Tubac, along with Father Font, set out to return to Mexico. The Tapia family, and especially Bartolo, were as sad to see them leave, as were the other colonists. Anza was a beloved leader. In his diary Anza writes "the tears they were shedding more because of my departure than of their exile, filling me with compassion. They showered me with embraces, best wishes, and praises which I do not merit."

Young Bartolo thrived on life in the crowded presidio, and with the other children spent time exploring the tide pools, hunting rabbits in the fields or helping with the family's horses. He often was responsible for the younger children. During this time he learned to read and write, as the Padres at the neighboring Mission Carmelo taught the little boys their catechism. Meanwhile the new commander, Lieutenant Jose Juaquin Moraga, awaited the arrival of the bark "San Carlos," bringing the supplies for Monterey presidio (where food was running short) and for the continuing expedition to San Francisco.

In a real fiesta on May 26, 1776 Bartolo's sister, Maria Antonia Tapia, was married at Mission Carmelo to José Antonio Buelna of Sinaloa. She was 14 years old. The young couple remained in Monterey to found their own family.

Just two days after the wedding, the group which had been left behind at San Gabriel, arrived in Monterey. What a joyful reunion all the colonists and soldiers had, exchanging stories of their journey up the coast! But with the influx of more people, plus more horses and cattle, the food problem at the Monterey presidio became really serious.

Bartolo was the first to see the white sails of the San Carlos as it hove into Monterey Bay. What a bustling two weeks, as supplies were unloaded for Monterey and Mission Carmel! The heavier travel-worn packs of the colonists were put on board. Finally everything was ready to the satisfaction of the lieutenant. The march to San Francisco began at 2P.M. on June 17, 1776, after mass at the mission. The long train slowly made its way out of Monterey - nearly 200 people and 300 head of cattle - some for the settlers and some for the new mission.

Just imagine the feelings of the people - leaving behind the final link with their culture and setting out into the unknown to make a completely new life for themselves. It must have been an exciting, as well as a fearful time - and the children surely reflected their elders' concerns. Being his father's eldest son, young Bartolo had some responsibility for the seven other Tapia children remaining with the train.

The walk to San Francisco was through country inhabited by many Indian villages. Some of the natives were friendly to the colonists and eager to receive the beads and trinkets the soldiers gave them. At this point they were not hostile to the newcomers - but surprised to see so many of them - especially women and children. Heretofore they had seen only the men of the various expedition groups. The Tapia children and their friends were as curious as the Indians, as they had enjoyed being with the Colorado River people.

The colonists came to the San Francisco area June 27, 1776 and made camp on the banks of the lagoon Anza had called "Nuestra Señora De Los Dolores." The soldiers and families pitched their threadbare tents and immediately set to work building a chapel of boughs. The first mass was celebrated in it June 29. Soon they built a rough-hewn chapel there and dedicated it to San Francisco de Asis. (It is today's Mission Dolores).

The natives couldn't contain their curiosity and came flocking around the camp. Many brought gifts of mussels and wild seeds and the colonists exchanged these for their food - which the Indians liked very much - except the milk - "which they refused to taste," Father Palou wrote.

The first settlers made do with tule-grass-roofed shelters walled with poles driven in the ground. Supplies ran critically short when the supply ship, San Carlos, did not arrive until August. A summer storm blew it clear back to San Diego from Monterey! Some foodstuffs came from Monterey in a smaller ship with neither clothing nor building materials aboard. By that time the people were in rags.

From August the work progressed and in early October the presidio and the mission were ready for the dedication. Settlers had more substantial dwellings and now had adequate food.

I found no record of Jose Bartolomeo during this period, but mission records show his father, Felipe Santiago Tapia and his stepmother, Juana Maria Cardenas, were parents of Maria Anacleta Tapia, born July 12, 1778 and baptized July 18, 1778 at Mission Santa Clara. Jose Bartolomeo was then 12 years old. Eventually there were four more children in the Felipe Tapia family, the last being Jose Casiano (Ursino) Tapia, whose baptismal date was August 8, 1786.

Jose Bartolomeo left home in 1782, the year he was 16. It was the custom in Mexico for the eldest son to join the army at that age. His first duty may have been as a soldier guard at Mission San Buenaventura. On November 14,1785 he was married to 13-year-old Maria Francesca Mauricia Villalobos at Mission San Buenaventura.

The young bride was born in 1772 at Villa Sinaloa, Mexico. Her parents were Juan Jose Miguel Villalobos of Sinaloa and Maria Nicolasa Beltran from San Miguel de Horcasitas, Mexico. Her father was a soldier at the pueblo of Los Angeles in 1781, and at the Mission Santa Barbara in 1785. He returned to Los Angeles and became a blacksmith there in 1792. Her mother died at Mission San Diego in 1792.

The newlywed couple remained for a time in San Buenaventura and the next written record of them is March 8, 1787, when their first child, Maria Tomasa Tapia, was baptized at Mission San Luis Obispo. (I found several reports saying Bartolo was mayordomo at San Luis Obispo in 1787.)

As mayordomo, Bartolo was "soldier missionary" and the manager-supervisor of all mission activities outside the spiritual. His job was to oversee the planting, the irrigating, the harvest of the fruits and vegetables. He had to make certain the animals were taken care of, and supervise the preparation of the hides and the wool. But even as steward of the mission, he was under the direction of the padres. The Tapias and their small daughter lived at the mission, as it was customary for the mayordomo to do.

Bartolo and Maria's second child, their first son, Tiburcio Tapia, was baptized April 14,1789 at Mission San Luis Obispo. Two years later, a third child, Maria Fernanda Tapia, was baptized May 31, 1791, also at San Luis Obispo. Sometime after Maria Fernanda's birth the young Tapias moved to the Pueblo de Los Angeles, for the California Pioneer Register and Index describes Bartolo Tapia as "ranchero at Los Angeles from 1791-1813."

California historian Hubert Howe Bancroft lists Bartolo Tapia among the seven who had "grants from the superior government" for ranchos or "sitios" for cattle raising. The records show Tapia as holding - in 1791 - "a sitio, besides two suertes and two gardens."

A sitio was "land for cattle raising." A suerte was a "piece of ground separated from the rest by bounds or landmarks." Could the "sitio" have been Rancho Topango Malibu Simi and Sequit? The suertes were two plots laid out within the four leagues of the Pueblo de Los Angeles, as were the gardens. I found evidence of this in Bartolo's last will and testament.

The Tapia's fourth child, Joseph Antonio Tapia, was baptized August 2, 1797 at Mission San Gabriel, there being no church in the Los Angeles pueblo at that time.

From the petition he wrote to Governor Jose Joaquin Arrillaga at Loreto, April 16, 1805, I knew Bartolo Tapia had received the Governor's permission to graze his livestock at "the place called 'Topango, Malibu, Simi Sequit." Don Felipe Goycoechea, Capitan Graduato and Commandant of the Garrison of Santa Barbara had granted this permission at the governor's order. In his petition Tapia asked the governor to evict a neighbor, Proguinto Suniga, who "for more than two years" has brought his mares and team horses there - interfering with Tapia's stock on the land granted to him.

Governor Arrillaga resolved the dispute with a message: "To the Commandant of the Garrison of Santa Barbara belongs the decision of this demand and that his order may be complied with in order that he who makes representation may be left in peaceable possession thereof. Arrillaga - Loreto, July 12, 1805."

In 1805 Bartolo's eldest son, Tiburcio, turned 16 and according to Spanish and Mexican custom, entered military service. He became a soldier and corporal of the Santa Barbara Company.

On the Malibu Rancho, Tapia's stock multiplied, reportedly to 6,000 cattle, horses and mares. There was a lively commerce in tallow and hides dragged down to the beach and put aboard ships for Mexico in exchange for goods and supplies for the family. Some also were transported to the Pueblo by oxcart. Old neighbors in the region of the Boca de Santa Monica rancho inferred that Tapia was engaged in smuggling operations. This was entirely possible, as under Spanish rule it was illegal for any Californian to have commerce with ships from anywhere but Mexico or Spain. By that time, the occasional Yankee vessel had come up the coast seeking trade.

In addition to the cattle raising on the Malibu Rancho, Tapia owned a vineyard in the Los Angeles Pueblo. (After his death more than thirty-five hundred plants were divided among his heirs). There also was a still with the necessary equipment, which on his death he bequeathed to his wife.

The Bartolo Tapia family lived in the Pueblo de Los Angeles, not at the Malibu rancho. That was strictly for grazing and cattle raising. There was a small wood house, some crude shelters and some corrals for the cattle, but "very little cultivation" according to an acquaintance. Tapia did stay at the rancho occasionally, as one of the ranch hands testified at the court hearing attempting to prove the ranch's ownership several years after Tapia's death. He said Tapia raised "wild cattle and gentle horses" at the ranch.

Tapia's daughter, Maria Tomasa, was married to Juan Jose Nieto on November 28, 1806 at Mission San Gabriel. The bridegroom, born in 1781, was the son of Manuel Nietos, part owner of the Nietos Rancho. There was a big fiesta to celebrate the wedding in true Spanish style.

Two years later - another wedding: On June 20, 1808 the second Tapia daughter, Maria Fernanda, became the bride of Eugenio Nicolas Alanis. Another fiesta!

Here records of Bartolo's life become sketchy. In his last will and testament made as he was dying – just before April 18, 1824 – he identifies himself as "lately a corporal of the artillery of the Royal Fort of San Diego." He states "with regard to the money which the King owes me by his paymaster" he asks his son, Tiburcio Tapia, to distribute "$1,000 amongst your brother and sisters." The remaining $1,000 or more was to go "to your mother." Both the mother and son were charged to give $150 to the mission "that they may say mass for the benefit of my soul"

In a postscript Bartolo remembers, "The sowed field shall remain to my wife for her subsistence." He describes the location of the field and adds "she shall have the still and two yokes of oxen, two pipes and three casks; also the images of the saints shall be 'for my old woman; the mill and the house.' Signed "Jose Bartolomeo Tapia" and then "the tract of the land and cattle is of my said wife." Guillermo Cota "certifies this to be a true statement in this testament" on April 18, 1824.

Four years later Bartolo's son, Tiburcio, makes an inventory which includes everything from a dozen cups, a white leather jacket, numerous harnesses and farm tools, his writing desk, 150 cattle, eight horses and one bell mare and colt, hatchets, two compasses, a pair of small pocket pistols, a traveling bag and a bag for "shoemaking business," two apple trees and four pear trees.

The tract of land with the cattle was the Malibu ranch, which Tiburcio managed for his mother until his death in 1845.

On January 24, 1848 she sold the rancho to her grandson-in-law, Leon Victor Prudhomme, for 400 pesos. He gave her 200 in cash and with the other 200 paid her grocery bill. Maria Francesca Mauricia Villalobos Tapia outlived all of her children. She died September 5, 1854 at the age of 83, and was buried in the Los Angeles Plaza.

There were many Tapias in California. Jose Bartolomeo Tapia came from a family of nine children born in Culiacán, Mexico. His father, Felipe Santiago Tapia, and his stepmother, Juana Cardenas, had six more children after they settled in the new San Francisco colony. Bartolomo was not the only Tapia to come to the pueblo of Los Angeles. In fact, several Tapias were living on the Malibu ranch when Prudhomme sold it to Matthew Keller in 1857. My story, "Lechuza" is about the wife of Augustin Tapia, one of Bartolo's grandsons.

Chapter 2

THE CHUMASH

Chumash civilization along the Malibu coastline was practically obliterated in the 200 years between the Anza Expedition of 1776 and the 1976 celebration of our country's founding. For more than 100 years there has been a consuming interest in these people and how they lived. Relics have been discovered in almost every square mile of Malibu soil. There have been close to 150 digs by various teams of archaeologists with much of the information still unpublished.

Archaeologists long ago discovered Chumash were artists: their rock paintings are remarkable; their carvings in steatite and serpentine outstanding in any museum today; their basketry equals any that has been discovered in the entire southwest. All of these art forms fascinate me because there are so many good examples in and from Malibu.

I had known about Chumash rock paintings for quite a while before I actually saw some, in a cave on private property, not too far from my home, I found them reasonably preserved.

This cave's surface is very rough and in some spots even "flakey". I saw several pictures of what seem to be antlered creatures. Others look like birds, and many large and small figures reminded me of flattened frogs. But by far the most unusual of all is a file of four horsemen wearing flat-topped hats. In his book *Rock Paintings of the Chumash,* Campbell Grant notes these are the only horses as well as the only figures in silhouette in any of the Chumash cave paintings.

Grant writes that when Juan Rodriguez Cabrillo landed in 1542 "the Chumash gave him excellent descriptions of armoured Spanish horsemen of Coronado's expedition seen in Arizona the previous year. News of these astonishing people had traveled to the coastal tribes through trade channels or by roving bands of Colorado River Mojaves..."

The hats are similar to the ones the padres wore, and diaries from the Anza expedition to San Francisco in 1776 tell that they traveled very near the location of this cave. I can imagine the Chumash shaman sitting upon the high rocks above this cave and watching the long procession of colonists, headed by the hat-wearing padres.

We do not know the real significance of these paintings to the natives. Because of the antlered creature, this cave may have been a ceremonial site for huntsmen. As the Chumash did not have writing, we shall never know.

I was introduced to another remarkable aspect of Chumash art when a friend, Doris, showed me her collection of artifacts discovered between 1939 and 1941 when the Roosevelt Highway through Malibu was widened.

The prize piece was a fish head carved from black stone. It may be the remains of a Chumash pipe. The stone (possibly serpentine) is polished to the smoothness of Italian marble. The fish's mouth is open, the lips nicely carved. Evidently the smoke exuded from the mouth opening. The eyes are carved from the stone, raised, and decorated with shell.

The gills are represented by groups of small white shell circles embedded in asphaltum growing narrower toward the mouth and widening as they go back. Here the piece is broken, showing the black stone was carved down to a thickness of only a quarter of an inch.

Doris' collection includes two small paint pots made from large fish vertebrae. The one lined with a shell that exactly fits has remnants of the ochre color paint around the edge. I held the perfect pelican head effigy and stroked the dark polished stone. It was as smooth as polished Italian marble. Doris thought some grooved stones might have been sinkers for a fish net. The many slender abalone fish hooks are sharp as any I have used. I could have cut my finger on the stone blade that still had its palm fiber handle attached with asphaltum. The skein of shell "money beads" rattled enticingly when I picked them up, and I was as enthralled as any Chumash young woman would have been when Doris showed me the bright red and blue glass trade beads. Both of us thought we'd bypass the finely polished bone hair ornament.

Doris loaned me a copy of *Inlaid Stone and Bone Artifacts from Southern California* by E. K. Burnett. This 1944 publication of the Museum of the American Indian Heye Foundation is filled with photographs of remarkable artifacts from Chumash burial sites in every canyon between Solstice and Sequit along the Malibu coastline. I was completely fascinated when the author noted all of the stone objects were fashioned solely with stone and bone tools. My sculptor husband used iron chisels and steel files to make the delicate horse ears in Italian marble. I marveled at the patience it must have required making these hollowed-out stone pipes with their tiny shell decorations with stone tools. I wanted to see the whole collection.

We were planning a trip east, so I wrote to the museum asking to see their collection from Malibu. We set a date and time and I eagerly appeared. But what a disappointment!

There was one large case labeled "Southwest Indians" full of a hodgepodge of artifacts, none of which were identified. There was no indication of any tribe at all. I recognized some Navajo things and looked carefully for something from Malibu but found nothing. I asked to see the Malibu collection depicted in the Burnett book and was told it was in the basement but I could not go down there as the staff was packing an exhibit to go to South America.

Since then in a newly constructed building the Smithsonian plans to exhibit Indian culture from all over North America. I wonder if the Chumash will be mentioned and if some of this wonderful collection will survive.

Doris gave her nice little collection to the Malibu Lagoon Museum. It too is under reconstruction at this writing (2004) and my concern is the same as for the other Chumash artifacts.

Chapter 3

WHERE DID THE CHUMASH GO?

In 1898, writing in *Happy Days in Southern California,* Frederick Hastings Rindge vividly describes life in an imaginary Chumash village on his Malibu rancho. As a well-read and widely traveled gentleman of his time, he was well acquainted with the current theories about "Whence came these people?" My concern now is "Where did they go?"

Archaeologists have estimated the native population of the Chumash roughly from Malibu Creek to Point Concepción, including the Channel Islands and inland to the mountains, as between 8,000 and 17,250 in the year 1770. A. L. Krober, the authority on California Indian life and languages, says the California Indian population as a whole declined nearly 90% from 1779 to 1910 and "in the case of the Chumash the decline was total."

My research led me to discover that between 1540 and 1542, native traders from inland tribes brought coastal people news of a strange group of creatures who had hairy faces and were the color of death, yet were shaped like the native Californians. Word of these beings who wore strange garments and carried many kinds of sticks (many very bright and shining); some of them sitting upon four-legged beasts that could run faster than the fastest messenger, spread throughout the southland - from the San Diego area up the coast to all of the islands.

One bright day some time later, island people saw on the ocean two canoes larger than any they had ever built. These canoes had tall white banners and went over the water with no paddlers. When the canoes drew near, the natives saw in them men like the strangers they had heard about.

The Spaniards (for these were Juan Cabrillo's ships exploring the California coast in 1542) were as interested in the natives as the natives were in them. This was a peaceful encounter. The natives exchanged fish for brightly colored beads and trinkets and allowed the seamen to secure fresh water for their journey. In pantomime, they described to the sailors the white men and their horses, about which the traders from the inland tribes had told them.

Of their exploration of the Santa Barbara Channel Islands, Juan Cabrillo in 1542-43 and Viscaino in 1602, wrote about being most impressed by the natives' seagoing canoes. Their crafts, made of wood planks literally sewn together, held as many as 12 paddlers. When they found no metal tools, the explorers were even more astonished at the fine wood bowls and basketry the natives brought to them.

The diarist describes the natives of the Santa Barbara Channel Islands as "well formed and of good body although not very corpulent" and he considered the women as "fairly good-looking." The men went naked except in cold weather, when they wore capes of animal skins.

A net around their waist held their stone knife and other small articles. Their hair was long and tied up with strings on which hung "geegaws of flint, bone, and wood."

Women wore modest knee-length skirts – one straight piece of animal skin in front and one in back, often fringed and ornamented with shell beads. In cold weather, women added a top covering fashioned from oblong rabbit, otter or sealskin tied together over one shoulder. Women wore their hair in short bangs in front, with short side locks, but long in back. A finely woven grass cap protected their heads when they carried packs.

Archaeologists have determined Chumash people lived in comparative peace in villages they called "rancherías." They were hunters and gatherers, and throughout present Malibu many of their grinding stones have been found. (One of these on our property beneath an oak tree.) Early diarists observed that in their Stone Age technology, the Chumash were superior to other natives further south. Chumash made efficient arrows and tools for cutting and scraping. Many of their skillfully woven, artistically decorated baskets remain on display in the Southwest Museum. They cut shells and drilled them with stone and bone tools, using these to decorate the steatite bowls, pipes and personal ornaments: earrings, necklaces and bracelets. Examples of these too are in museums – some even in the Musée de L'Homme in Paris.

Stories told by old informants and diaries of mission priests indicate the Chumash had a richly spiritual religion. They believed in an upper world where the sun, moon, and stars lived. A middle world – supported by two giant serpents that are moving about causing earthquakes — was home to the "First People," supernatural humans and animals. After their creation the Chumash lived in the middle world. Supernatural beings dangerous to man lived in a lower world.

I read that each person in Chumash times had a "dream helper," revealed in a tolocahe-induced trance at a sacred ritual. That dream helper determined the person's rank in the society – the eagle, thunder, or bear being more significant (powerful) than say the rabbit or the mouse. Throughout life, the dream helper — if all of the proper rituals were observed — literally guided the individual in every action.

Even the latest informants said the most powerful person in the Chumash order of things was the shaman. He healed the sick and controlled the climate with the proper rituals to keep the world in balance. If he failed, the time was wrong, the gods were angry, or more ceremonials had to be performed. The shaman presided at all ceremonies: puberty rites for boys and girls (where their dream helper was revealed to them), summer and winter solstices, burials, and other events. He was responsible for keeping the world in balance, teaching the youth, and reminding and encouraging the adults the best way to behave in their environment and with their gods. He was both feared and revered by everyone and his word was law, even above the chief.

Over the thousands of years they lived along the California coast, the Chumash seem to have adjusted their lives admirably to fit their environment. There was no discernible change in their habits in the more than 200 years between the explorations of Cabrillo and Viscaino and the land excursion of Gaspar de Portola in 1769.

I believe the legend of the white men in the big canoes that went over the sea with no paddlers was passed down through the generations in Chumash lore. The bright bead and shiny trinket gifts from the sailors were treasured until finally all were lost in the sand or had rusted away. The Indians really were not too surprised to see white men return on their horses. Whether in awe or in dread of them, one of the Chumash artists (a Malibu shaman?) painted on the wall of a rock shelter in the Malibu mountains a line of four horsemen wearing hats resembling those worn by the friars.

Chumash life changed in the 18th century. Spaniards came to California to set up a chain of missions and presidios when the King of Spain needed to hold the land from both Russia and England. The first mission was founded in San Diego in 1769. Coming up the coast the fathers established San Carlos Borromeo in 1770 and San Antonio de Padua and San Gabriel Archangel both in 1771. These were close to Chumash territory but did not infringe on their rancheriás.

Then, as I have written in Chapter One, Juan Bautista de Anza's second expedition in 1776 brought the first families of settlers to California from Mexico by way of the southern deserts. As I mentioned, they stopped at Mission San Gabriel en route to San Francisco. Pedro Font, one of the diarists with the expedition, kept a complete journal of the trip. His description of the territory makes me sure that from the San Gabriel Mission they journeyed across what is now San Fernando Valley and stopped overnight at the hidden spring at Las Virgenes. Of the 21 missions established between 1769 and 1823 five were in Chumash territory.

From the beginning, each mission had to be self supporting. Mexico and the "home base" were months away either by land or sea. The entire founding personnel of a mission might consist of two or three padres, anywhere from 15 to 35 "leatherjacket soldiers" (soldados de cuero) and their officers plus the families of a few of the soldiers. They brought some cattle, some seeds to plant, the barest essentials of food, and some tools, along with the germs of their diseases. The missionaries' zeal to convert the natives was doubled by their need of help to build, plant, sow, herd, and reap.

Without the Indians, the missions would have been impossible. After a few incidents, the Chumash remained relatively docile and began to come to the missions, where they learned building and horticultural skills, along with the principles of Christianity. Father Geiger, in describing the building of Mission Santa Barbara, mentioned that any of the soldiers who knew a trade served as teachers to the Indians. One soldier showed them how to make and lay adobe bricks, another taught them to do stone work, another the process of tanning, weaving, etc. Very often the padres themselves taught the Indians and worked right along with them.

Chumash life as recounted by informants whose parents or grandparents lived it "in the old way" seems to have been an idyllic pastoral existence. I often wonder why these people would abandon it for the missions.

Then I remind myself most had never before seen shiny beads the colors of spring flowers. They had never felt the softness of cloth as compared to tanned animal skins and woven grass. They had never imagined a gleaming steel knife that would stay sharp longer than their sharpest obsidian ones. Accustomed to their own talismans, they would have been fearfully intrigued by the strangers' odd talisman of crossed sticks and must have been completely captivated by the sound of the mission bells. Accustomed to their rock art pictures, they would have been more than interested in the priests' pictures of the Virgin Mary whom they were told was the mother of the god the padres worshipped. The most sophisticated shaman must have wondered at the power of these things and if they might be a serious threat to him. Since human nature is really spelled "C-U-R-I-O-S-I-T-Y" some of the venturesome did go to the missions.

As early as 1785, mission records at San Buenaventura list the baptism of a man from Humaliwu. In his research for the *Aboriginal*

Population of the Santa Barbara Channel Alan K. Brown's records between 1785 and 1801 show a total of 309 baptisms from Humaliwu He considered this the coastal area east from Mugu to Malibu Creek. It is the most remote of any of the inhabited places along the coast. The mountains come right down to the sea everywhere except at the mouths of creeks where there are lagoons. Any flatland ends in abrupt cliffs and the only way into the entire area is by tortuous mountain trails or by canoe on the ocean - and as the name implies - the surf is high. But archaeological evidence indicates the people of prehistoric Humaliwu had a culture much the same as those of the Santa Barbara and the Channel Islands.

As far as I know, no research has established how many of the "gentiles" (unconverted Indians) remained unconverted. They became "neophytes" (were baptized) only after they were instructed. Gentiles lived and worked at the missions, converting when they were ready. Some never were. In the earliest mission times some of the diaries tell of mass conversions and mass baptisms performed by sprinkling a whole crowd with holy water.

Fr. Vicente de Santa Maria traveled overland from Ventura to Los Angeles in 1795 searching for a site for a new mission (which turned out to be Mission San Fernando, established in 1797). He wrote in his journal that he saw Indians building a limekiln near a Spanish rancho and working as "Cowherds, cattlemen, irrigators, bird catchers, foremen, and horsemen." He also saw Indians cultivating watermelons, sugar melons, and corn. He wrote "the whole of pagandom between this mission (Buenaventura) and that of San Gabriel along the beach, along the Camino Real and along the border of the north is fond of the Pueblo of Los Angeles, of the Rancho of Verdugo, of the Rancho of the Reyes, and the zanja irrigation ditch. Here we see nothing but pagans passing, clad in shoes with sombreros and blankets, and serving as muleteers to the settlers and rancheros, so that if it were not for the gentiles there would be neither pueblo nor rancho."

Father Geiger mentions "dry years" between 1787 and 1802. It was difficult to find enough water for Mission Santa Barbara. I am sure this drought affected the Chumash natural way of life. When there isn't enough rain, chía does not bloom, islay does not produce fruit, yuccas are small, and life is hard for all animals. This may have been a reason for some of the Indians quitting the mission to go to the ranchos to work in exchange for food, clothing, a few beads, and a knife or other trinket.

The ranchería of Humaliwu, archaeologists believe, was on the east side of Malibu Creek - about a mile from where Jose Bartolomeo Tapia constructed his rancho buildings. Based on Father Vicente's remarks, Tapia no doubt had some of the Indians working for him and paid them with glass beads. Archaeologist Virginia F. G. Bickford did research on the Chumash cemetery in Humaliwu where thousands of glass beads were discovered along with the traditional Chumash "money beads."

Bickford mentions "a degree of influence exerted by the Spanish on traditional Indian lifestyles" which she infers from a list of metal buttons, an iron concho, a new St. Francis medal daubed with ochre and a pair of metal shoe buckles along with remnants of Spanish saddle trappings, a Spanish bridle ornament and a star rowel and heel plates from a Spanish spur. Blades of steel knives that had been hafted to bone or wood with asphaltum also were found, along with pieces from a flintlock rifle and a sword "from weapons typical of the latter half of the 18th century." This person could have been a vaquero — although the grave may have contained remains of several — Bickford does not elaborate.

As far as actual documentation from any of the owners of Rancho Topango Malibu Simi and Sequit, it is as if the Chumash did not exist.

We do not know if Humaliwu ranchería's population lived in tule grass houses. We do not know if all of them or only a few were enticed into the mission world, as not everyone was baptized. We do not know if any of the Christianized Chumash ever came back to Humaliwu. The finding of the St. Francis medal daubed with ochre says eloquently to me this person's relatives were "covering all bases" and invoking the old way (in which ochre was a substance used in spiritual rituals) and the new (with the St. Francis medal).

Rindge mentions in his book, "The padres at San Gabriel used to send their Indians to the Malibu Ranch to fish and hunt, drying the fish and venison for a winter's supply." This is the only historical record I have come across about Indians in Malibu.

However, in 1968 Bobbie Sanders, my amateur archaeologist friend, uncovered a primitive burial ground beside Trancas Creek. The sight of people digging in the field attracted the attention of her Malibu neighbors and the County Sheriff, just as Bobbie unearthed a perfectly preserved skull. The sheriff told Bobbie he had to take the skull to the L.A. County Coroner's office for investigation, and that he would return it later.

Her Malibu neighbors became the Malibu Archaeological Society and received written permission from the property owners to continue the dig. In the meantime, Bobbie had no word from either the sheriff or the County Coroner. Eventually she found out from the sheriff the investigation was complete — there was no murder involved and the bones were not of interest. Because they had no further use for them (to her dismay) they cremated the bones.

The Malibu Archaeological Society continued to dig, revealing 14 burials. Word spread of the Trancas dig. John Beaton and Nelson Leonard of UCLA and the Archaeological Survey got themselves into the act. Finally the whole dig went to UCLA and in the Survey Annals is labeled 4-Lan-197. In all there were 104 burials.

Possibly because this particular civilization was not as advanced as the later Chumash, the only artifacts discovered were one mortar, one pestle, a couple of projectile points, some flaked stones, and one small ochre mortar. This later was filched from John Beaton's desk at UCLA. Nothing ever was done with those bones by 1981 — I saw them in a drawer in the UCLA archaeological department then.

Bobbie Sanders says 97% of the Trancas burials were fully extended, 70% were on the back, 24% were face down and 6% were lying on the right side. Heads were toward the ocean and feet toward the mountain.

It would have been interesting to know the carbon dating of these bones, how the people met their death, were there discernible diseases, evidence of broken or bashed in bones, etc. Unfortunately we'll never know, unless some archaeological student at UCLA wishes to further the investigation.

Chapter 4

LA LECHUZA

When my friend Merritt Adamson was being a bratty little boy, his nanny would tell him "La Lechuza will get you." Lechuza was the "Owl Woman" in Californio legend, equivalent to the "Boogey Man" of my midwest childhood.

Unlike my midwest Boogey Man, there was a real live Lechuza in Malibu's early days. I pieced her tale together out of my search through thousands of pages of testimony in the Prudhomme-Keller case for the title to Rancho Malibu and in the May K. Rindge case about the highway through Malibu. Here is her story:

When Don Mateo Keller purchased Rancho Topango Malibu Simi and Sequit from Leon Victor Prudhomme in 1857, several members of the Tapia family remained on the rancho, claiming it by right of inheritance. Among these were Augustine Tapia, grandson of Bartolomeo Tapia, and his wife, Jesus de Tapia – known as "Lechuza."

How this woman fell heir to the name – a Spanish nickname for "persons resembling owls in any of their qualities" I do not know. One of her contemporaries, J.J. Carrillo, defined "Lechuza" as "night owl."

At first I thought perhaps she traveled around the ranch by night. Maybe she had amber eyes (the color of owl eyes) or an owlish face with big round eyes. Or did the nickname come from the canyon near where she lived – "Lechuza?" I remembered an old map of Rancho Malibu where the canyon between "Little Alisos" (Decker) and "Ensenal" (Encinal) is marked "Lechuza." A small square near the ocean and close to this canyon is marked "Lechuza's house." Spellings vary from La Chuza, Luchuza, Lachuza to Lechusa. No matter, for Lechuza was a real person and her house was a landmark for those who made the journey up the coast from Santa Monica to Ventura or Santa Barbara.

Lechuza was dressed in men's clothes, carrying "a big gun on the side and riding astride a large horse" the day in 1872 young Juan Salgado came up to her house looking for a stray mule. He told the court "she looked pretty tough." Salgado spotted the mule among a band of horses one of Lechuza's sons was looking after, just as Lechuza rode up. When he explained to her the mule belonged to the government, she sent him on his way with the creature – back down the coast by way of Santa Monica Canyon to Los Angeles.

In the Rindge trial, Antonio Reyes, son of the late Ysidro Reyes, said he stopped to talk with Lechuza's husband when he and Francisco Valenzuela were on their way to Triumpho Canyon to the north. Andrés Olivera, J.J. Ramirez, and Juan Jose Pena said they were among the travelers making their way along the Malibu Rancho to Ventura who stopped at Lechuza's house.

When he was 17 or 18 (in 1863) Pasqual Martinez said he made the journey by oxcart from his father's Santa Monica Ranch on the coast about six miles east of Malibu to Lechuza's house past Suma (Dume) to get beans. He explained Mexican oxcarts had solid wooden wheels about four inches thick and the "road" was on the beach most of the way. The Tapia family hauled out wool in their carreta hitched to a pair of burros, according to Thomas I. Moffett, another contemporary.

Neighbors said Lechuza raised beans, pumpkins, corn, watermelons, and other things and that she and her sons took this produce into town along the beach "road" in a horse-drawn wagon.

Lechuza's daughter, Antonia, married Antonio Valdez and both of them remained at her mother's house. Señor R. Pico rode through the Malibu Rancho in 1875 looking for suitable grazing ground for his horses and talked with Valdez.

Young Reginaldo Tapia said he and his friends nicknamed Lechuza as "The Cahuenga." He did not translate the word in his testimony so I do not know whether this Shoshonean name was meant to be kind or impertinent.

By 1869 Lechuza was a widow, but she still lived in the adobe house on the mesa with her six children and host of Tapia relatives that came and went on horseback with packhorses to carry the provisions.

She was known as "The old woman who lived there at Lechuza." When her wagon broke down, Geraldo Bojorquez (who lived in a brush hut in Suma and was another claimant to the Malibu Ranch) loaned her his wagon so she could get provisions.

At some time during his term in office (1872- 76) Los Angeles County Sheriff William O. Rowland paid a visit to the Lechuza place. He found only the adobe house, no wagons, stable or outbuildings. Had a raging brush fire destroyed them?

In 1876 the Tapia family lost their suit against Matthew Keller to claim the Rancho Topango Malibu Simi and Sequit and all of them left the ranch. From May 1879 until the following year, A. H. Dunlap and his brother grazed 600 cattle on the Malibu. They camped at Lechuza's for two months. The house was empty.

Today the Lechuza adobe has returned to the earth from which it was made. But about five miles up Encinal Canyon Road from Pacific Coast Highway – where Encinal turns to the right – you may pass a stretch of road one-tenth of a mile long leading straight to Decker Canyon Road – "Lechusa Road."

Chapter 5

FILMING

It is an unusual day in Malibu when you can drive along the 27-mile stretch of beach, into some of the canyons, or along the top of one of the mesas, without seeing at least one film company "on location." Filming is just part of the "Malibu way of life."

Over coffee several years ago at his Decker Canyon Ranch, Raymond Goodson alerted my curiosity when he mentioned he was stationed to guard both the Malibu Ranch and the Warner Brothers Film Company in 1926.

The first time any movie company had ever been permitted to work inside the rancho was the summer May K. Rindge gave Warner Brothers permission to use her Malibu Beach as the setting for their film "Across the Pacific." Goodson, a member of the Los Angeles County Motor Patrol, was hired to watch over the property.

"The real sensation," Goodson told me, "was to get into Malibu". All other people were stopped at the Las Flores gates. Members of the company were permitted to pass freely back and forth, but nobody else. Goodson had no problems whatsoever with anyone during the whole course of his duty.

Gently curving Malibu Beach was, in 1926, pristine in every sense of the word: "Of or pertaining to the earliest period; primitive; having its original purity; uncorrupted or unsullied." Until the film company moved in and set up its props, there was nothing on Malibu Beach but the shining white sand and a few skeins of seaweed left to dry in the sun by the last high tide.

Photos from the archives of the Academy of Motion Picture Arts and Sciences show that when the Warner Brothers set designers finished their job, Malibu Beach had undergone a transformation into their idea of the tropics, complete with literally hundreds of artificial palm trees. One row of these trees stretched the length of the beach, as far as the camera's eye could see. A line of regulation U.S. Army tents faced the ocean--enough of them to house a complete battalion of actor-soldiers.

Goodson told me quite a few stayed all night in these tents part of the time the company remained on location. There were more than 300 people in the entire shooting company. The mess tent where everyone ate, was set up well off the beach on the site of the present Malibu Plaza shopping center.

Across the Pacific starred Monte Blue and Jane Winton, with co-stars Walter McGrail and Myrna Loy. The play was written by Charles Blaney and was adapted for the film by Darryl F. Zanuck. Ray Del Ruth directed, with Byron Haskin as photographer. The movie was released in October, 1926.

The picture opened at Loew's in New York on November 4, 1926. *Variety* described it as "a fast moving mellerdrammer in the style of the

'Injun Cowboy' pictures of 10 years ago." Uncle Sam's "doughboys" fought a gang of rebel Filipinos attempting to throw off the yoke of constitutional law and order shortly after the Spanish-American War. Actress Jane Winton played the part of Monte Blue's sweetheart. Myrna Loy, in the part of the "brown-skinned maiden," fell in love with the hero and finally exposed the rebel leader. The picture ended in a regularly planned war — all on Malibu Beach more than 75 years ago.

Chapter 6

A Highway Runs Through It

In 1949, when my husband and I came to live on the beach in Malibu, the Pacific Coast Highway was a three-lane road. This was "Before Freeways" and trucks from Northern California came barreling down the road at all hours of the day and especially at night. In those days people didn't live in Malibu many months before the subject of May K. Rindge's years-long battle to keep the highway from going through her 27-mile rancho came up for discussion.

My curiosity was aroused and I began to put together all of the "bits and pieces" I had read about. I went clear back to the beginning:

Malibu's mountains literally have their feet in the ocean. In prehistoric times the Chumash and Gabrileño Indians and their predecessors would have traveled on foot along the beach's wet, hard sand. Up on the mesas and down in the canyons, the hunters could follow deer trails.

In the early 1800s Jose Bartolomeo Tapia, Rancho Malibu's first owner, brought necessary supplies over the mountains via the rugged Calabasas trail from the Pueblo Los Angeles, where most of his interests were. He may have ridden his horse along the wet sandy beach when he visited the adjoining Rancho Boca de Santa Monica. His neighbors told of transporting hides in oxcart "carretas" from the ranch to the beach for loading on ships for Mexico (Note: Richard Henry Dana in *Two Years Before the Mast* describes how the sailors and laborers carried the hides through the surf to rowboats, and from there threw the hides up to the sailors in the ships to stash below decks).

A later owner of Rancho Malibu, Don Mateo Keller, regularly used the rough and rocky beach route from Santa Monica to his property. In 1875 he filed a petition to the Los Angeles County Board of Supervisors offering to dedicate a public highway from Santa Monica across his rancho to Malibu Lake (shown on an early map as being close to the present Malibu Lagoon).

The supervisors appointed "viewers" who looked at the plans for the project and recommended the adoption of the petition and the immediate improvement of the rugged road. The only flaw in the arrangement was the fact that Keller did not own any land beyond the eastern border of his ranch and had no authority to offer a right-of-way for a public road from there to Santa Monica. The project was dropped.

Messrs. Harris and Guthrie, who in 1874 had come over the Ventura Mountains to claim government land adjoining the western border of Rancho Malibu, drove a two-horse wagon from Santa Monica clear across the Malibu Rancho to their place. (It must have been in the fall when the tides are the lowest, the sand the hardest). Even so, they must have had to drive their horses "up and over" at many places, such as Point Dume, Carbon Point and Big Rock. I don't know how many days the trip lasted. Some early photographs show that even the Rindges had to pull up to higher ground to wait the tide's ebb before continuing the drive along the beach.

There must have been considerable travel up and down the beach and through Rancho Malibu because Frederick Hastings Rindge had to put up gates at the east entrance to his rancho (at Las Flores Canyon). Even though he gave keys to the settlers who lived beyond the ranch, some refused to accept them and had him cited before the Board of Supervisors. Thus began the 33 years of litigation over the road.

Thousands of words have been written about Mr. Rindge's widow, May Knight Rindge, and her battles in one court after another, up to and including the United States Supreme Court, in her attempt to keep the highway from going through her ranch. She even offered land along the upper border of the ranch instead of the sought-after beach right-of-way. No deal. She lost. On April 16, 1919, Los Angeles County was given the right-of-way through Rancho Malibu for the highway.

I was able to get the report of California Highway's resident engineer, C.P. Montgomery. It goes into detail with facts and figures about the construction of Pacific Coast Highway from its beginning in Santa Monica to its end at Arroyo Seco, the west boundary of Rancho Malibu.

By 1921 the rugged dirt road from Santa Monica to Las Flores was paved with concrete twenty feet wide and six inches thick. But it was 1926 before the roadbed for the 16.3 miles between Las Flores and Arroyo Seco was completed. Even so it was just a dirt road, no paving.

The route through Rancho Malibu was not easy. Over 125 gullies had to have special construction; several large culverts had to have temporary crossings; a few canyons needed reinforced concrete bridges. The state highway engineers built the ones at Malibu Creek, Solstice Canyon and Corral Canyon in 1925 and 1926. Los Angeles County was to build the other five.

Then in 1926 and 1927 came the first concrete paving on the six-plus miles between Las Flores and Latigo Canyons. Real problems this time: The region was inaccessible by road or rail so all materials had to be trucked from a special plant near the Santa Monica city limits served by the Pacific Electric Railroad Line. All the water was piped in from a Los Angeles County supply three miles north of Santa Monica and trucked to the highway work place. The shortest haul to the work site was about seven miles, the longest over thirteen.

From Winter Canyon (the current location of Webster School and Our Lady of Malibu Catholic Church) to Latigo Creek, the center line of the roadway actually followed the center line of the Rindges' abandoned Hueneme, Malibu, and Southern Railroad along the beach. I also thought it interesting that in several places the old embankment had to be widened to 40 feet. (Parts of this road remain as Old Malibu Road in the same location behind houses on the beach.) The stretch of road near Corral Canyon needed too many fills for concrete, so it was paved with "macadam." Two-foot rock borders five inches thick lined this portion.

Several severe spring storms during construction carried nearly half of the roadway out to sea. Between the old Malibu wharf (at about the present site of Malibu pier) and Malibu Creek the sea came overland more than 600 feet. The engineers had to haul 8,000 tons of rock to protect the roadway there.Another controversy in 1925 over a stand of ancient oaks and sycamores at Solstice Canyon was finally settled out of court three years later. Finally, on June 26, 1929, the gates that had protected the unpaved portion of the highway were removed and the motoring public was permitted to drive through Malibu.

Herve Babineau came to Malibu over the new road in 1929. He remembered it as "good." He drove a Plymouth Club coupe and said the road was "fine clear to Ventura." But he did remember that beyond Latigo Canyon the road still was a temporary oil and rock pavement.

Harvey Anderson came to work in Malibu in 1930 and lived in a shack at the top of Latigo Canyon. His memories were of a winding road along the Latigo shore. He told me there was so much slippage the waterlines were above ground. Slabs of the original concrete are still a part of the present Latigo Shore Road in 2003.

By 1933 the road, now named "Roosevelt Highway," was being widened from "Beverly Boulevard" (which must have been Sunset Boulevard where it comes to the beach) to Las Flores Canyon. The bridge over Topanga Creek was widened. This was in the midst of the depression, and by law the contractor had to get all of his common labor from lists of the Los Angeles County Employment Stabilization Bureau. Only skilled labor could be hired from anywhere else in the State of California.

Add another problem: the Santa Monica section of this highway was in trouble over the Palisades Beach Road below famed Palisades Park. The bluff kept slipping and engineers were scratching their heads trying to find a solution. Over the years, several houses at the top of the bluff have been removed and gigantic protective bulkheads installed along the highway, but even today (2004) the palisades remain unstable.

Automobiles improved, more people were driving, and in 1926 there had to be a change at Walnut Creek, just west of Ramirez Canyon. There a new bridge crossed the canyon and today residents have to drive under the highway to get to their homes. The improvements went as far as Encinal Canyon with new bridges across Zuma and Trancas creeks. Now the 80-foot-wide highway also had a divider strip in the center.

Next the work began on the most difficult part of the road – to eliminate the much washed-out section along Latigo Shore and around the point. This meant crossing the gigantic "railroad slide" where, years before, the whole mountain had come down between Corral and Latigo Canyons.

Engineers discovered an 80-foot deep pocket of sand on the slide 90 feet above the highway. This sand was covered with a 20-foot cap of volcanic breccia. All of this had to be removed. First a ramp road had to be built so that the power shovels (predecessors of today's earth moving behemoths) could drive up to the sand. The breccia had to be very carefully dynamited so as not to create more sliding. The engineers were able to use all of this material in the roadbed, however, saving a lot of hauling.

That year, 1936, a series of winter storms took out the roadway along Latigo Shore, so it was rerouted up over the hill just in front of the Gull's Way estate gates. This served until 1946 when a massive reconstruction began. The new road took off across the flat land behind Malibu Colony and up over the hill. The old highway still is in use as Old Malibu Road.

John Merrick brought his family to live on Latigo Shore Road in 1945. He remembered the construction work at the junction of the old and new roads as a "messy, muddy place." When the bulldozers started to work on the dirt, John borrowed Tom Doyle's jeep to haul loads of topsoil to his beach and made a good garden.

The site of the present Malibu Plaza mall now covers the early Malibu business section – with the Malibu Inn and Market, Louis Busch's real estate office, Andy Anderson's gas station (sold to George and Honey Coatsworth in 1946). Most of the houses there were demolished when the road changed. The Busch Real Estate office, the gas station and Malibu Inn relocated when main traffic no longer passed by.

In 1949 the highway through Malibu from Topanga was a three-lane road. Truck traffic roared by at all hours and it was worth my life to make a left turn to the beach house parking space. But by 1955 the three-lane road was history. There were marked turnouts at major intersections. But the "frosting on the cake" for us beach-dwellers: the addition of center turnout lanes.

It is hard to tell which is the more anxiety-provoking, fires or mudslides? The worst of the latter has ended (for now) with the removal of three houses above Las Flores Canyon Road and the reconfiguring of that entire bluff with a myriad of drains and reinforcements.

Several years ago a movement began to bring a freeway from San Fernando Valley out through Malibu Canyon to Pacific Coast Highway. Malibu stopped it cold before proposed plans could be completed. In 2003 with every new subdivision from even as far away as Simi Valley the highway traffic increases as the newcomers figure, "It's only an hour from work. Let's move to the country!"

I wonder what is next for our Pacific Coast Highway!

Chapter 7

MALIBU FIRES

A rainbow of wildflowers and chaparral blooming in mounds of brilliant white and blue over the whole mountainside greeted us for our first springtime in Malibu. My friend Roberta's comment, "Fuel for another big fire," seemed dour at the time, but didn't dampen my enthusiasm. After a few years in Malibu I learned she was right. Fire IS a fact of life here.

No one knew this better than retired Fire Chief Harvey Anderson. He joined the Los Angeles County Fire Department in 1931, fresh out of UCLA with a degree in botany and zoology. With his shovel and ax in the back of his 1926 truck, Harvey's duty began at the Escondido Station, up Latigo Canyon. Then Malibu was a working cattle ranch, unpopulated except for a few cottages near Malibu Creek. At $4 per day, seven days a week, Harvey went around quenching brush fires before they became conflagrations, thus learning all the mountain roads in the area.

His first command, in 1933, was the Quail Lake station on the Ridge Route. He married Alice Chambers and two of their four children were born there. His next command was Topanga, where he remained until his mandatory retirement in 1968.

But he only was 65 years old and in good health. As he looked around at his co-workers, he saw most of them really out of condition and not physically prepared for the strenuous activity of fighting brush fires. SO – he convinced the powers-that-be to start a fitness program for the entire force! This program is still in effect. We regularly see groups of firemen walking and running on Zuma Beach and along Mulholland Highway.

Harvey finally retired at age 80, and died at age 91 (in 1999). Through his long life he considered every day a celebration of being alive and followed his grandfather's advice, "Help every man you can and it will come back to you ten times over."

One day shortly before he died, Harvey told me about the first Malibu fire he worked. It began at Lake Sherwood on October 23, 1935. With the dreaded Santa Ana winds blowing gale force, this blaze joined the Latigo Canyon-Las Flores fire already burning. The Latigo Mountain Inn, lunch stop for people traveling from San Fernando Valley to the beach, was a major casualty. Harvey said the firemen cut back the chaparral as fast as they could, but the fire burned faster. Hard work shoveling dirt and chopping brush finally conquered the blaze before any more structures were damaged. He remembered the intense heat of working without modern protective gear.

Fire succeeded fire — 1938, 1941, 1948, 1953 – then came a "big one". It started in Newton Canyon the night of December 25, 1956 and burned for five days, searing all of Malibu down to Las Flores Creek. More than 50 homes were destroyed and one young man, Frank Dickover, was killed.

The Big Rock area escaped in 1956, but three years later, on December 31, the fire that had started behind Malibu burned down onto the highway through Big Rock. I had steaks defrosting on the kitchen counter for our New Year's Eve party with friends from Oregon. We heard sirens and saw flashing red lights headed down the highway. Our friends took off to Santa Monica to get through to relatives before the road was closed. We safely evacuated our horses from Serra Canyon and close to midnight, still in our fire fighting jeans, were the only New Year's Eve diners in Mr. Brown's elegant Rendezvous Restaurant, just a short walk from our Carbon Beach home.

The 1970 fire still gives me nightmares. It began Friday, September 25, with a gust of searing wind, a sprinkle of ashes in a swimming pool and an ominous cloud of smoke in the northeast above the mountains behind our Carbon Canyon horse farm. Those soaring flames, hot wind, burning ash, screaming fire sirens and flashing red lights still haunt me when the Santa Ana winds begin.

That night our concern was our show horses at the bottom of threatened Carbon Canyon. My husband, Ed, herded them down to the vacant lot next to our house on the beach and tied them to the fence. My job was to keep 10 spooked creatures from breaking the ties. Our friend Lisle Schweitzer drove up with our trailer, and took two of the beasts to safety at Hollywood Park.

Came another Good Samaritan in the form of a man with his ten fingers already bandaged from burns. He drove a four-horse trailer and not only offered four horses a ride to Hollywood Park, but came back for three more. And I never ever knew his name.

I was left with the wildest one, an old gelding who jumped every time a wave hit the beach.

I later found my problems a mere nothing compared to so many others throughout Malibu as one home after the other in Malibu Knolls caught fire. On Old Malibu Road, chimneys stood over masses of rubble, marking a line of homes; Malibu's famous landmark, Serra Retreat, left standing there on its hill – just a pile of smoldering rubbish.

Even so, there were a few lighter moments: Tim Walston dumped a drawer of socks into a suitcase, put his tax records into a paper bag, rounded up his wife, the St. Bernard, the German shepherd and the family cat and stood ready to evacuate his Grayfox Drive home in the Corvair. He didn't have to.

Schiller Colberg literally gave the shirt off his back to the clothing center set up at the Malibu Presbyterian Church. Later I found his custom-made cuff links to prove it. That was the beginning of "The Artifact Tree", where Honey Coatsworth got the idea, and founded Malibu's thrift shop, still (in 2004) doing a thriving business.

Alice Kling described her amusement at overhearing a woman sightseer say "Poor Mrs. Kling, lost in the fire. I didn't know her, but..." At that point one of Alice's horse-owner renters interrupted with introductions to her all around. Alice never did find out how the obituary ended.

We noticed our myoporum trees seemed to be fire retardant. A bunch of them saved the wood rails on our riding ring. Bobbie Sanders of Gardenland sent out a list of fire retardant plants with good root systems to prevent after-the-fire erosion. Gardenland and Calvin's Nursery escaped the fire, as did Bowman's Violet Greenhouse.

Driving down the California Street Incline in Santa Monica on my way home from town October 23, 1978 I saw that dreaded dark billowing cloud over the mountains. Another fire in Malibu? Now we were living in the mountains! I broke every speed limit on PCH and arrived at Encinal Canyon Road just as a sheriff in a yellow Ventura County car had adamantly closed the road. I turned around and headed for Kanan-Dume where I did get through. I could see the smoke rising higher and higher as I tore through the tunnels and down to Mulholland. That road was still open. I saw the tower of smoke getting bigger and bigger but the fire hadn't come over the ridge. So far, so good.

But when I got to the intersection of Mulholland and Westlake Boulevard, another Ventura County sheriff stopped me dead, in spite of my entreaties and those of Sheila Edwards, a neighbor whose house we could see from where we stood. What to do? My husband didn't know where I was or whether I had gotten through. This intersection was within walking distance from our house on Mulholland. Though I did my best, that sheriff would not let me through. So I drove back down Mulholland to Arch Oboler's house and banged on his door. Nobody heard me over the music playing somewhere inside.

Back again to the corner. When a fireman came by with a walkie-talkie, I asked him to connect me with our friend Tom Doyle, whose call number I remembered. He made the connection with Tom. I asked him to call Ed and tell him where I was stranded. He succeeded, and after about 45 minutes, up came Ed Stotsenberg running along Mulholland, even though it had been closed the first time I came by.

We decided I should try to get home via Encinal where it connected with Mulholland, even though it was closed the first time I tried to pass. Ed turned around and ran home, over the protests of the sheriff, who did not try to run and catch him!

This time there was no barricade at Mulholland/Encinal. The fire had already burned through. As I passed still smoldering bushes along the road, smoke stung my eyes and throat even though the car windows were closed. Finally I made it home! I leapt into my jeans and sweatshirt, ready to man the pump in the pool and spray the shrubbery in case of necessity. Miraculously the wind changed so the fire didn't come up across our bare fields. But it still burned. The next morning we watched women from the Civilian Conservation Corps (CCC) put out flames creeping up a small hill across Little Sycamore Road from us.

The fire in 1985 was a different story. We were running in a track meet in Rome. The big news there was the Achille-Lauro disaster. That panicked some, but our travel agent told us to continue our vacation to Florence, Venice and Athens as planned. On a phone call in Athens, Ed's secretary told him "The good news is that you house did not burn." He asked for the bad news, and it was bad for many people in Malibu. When we came home in late July, our house stood in the middle of a mountainside of charred sticks and ashes that extended clear back to Lake Sherwood, where the fire began as a "controlled burn."

Another disastrous fire hit Malibu in 1994, burned most of the homes on Las Flores. Up here on Mulholland that fire scared us too. My computer, the scrapbooks of track meets around the world and precious business papers went into the trunk of my car. My practical husband piled clothes into the trunk of his. We parked both down on Mulholland along with our neighbors from several miles around. For three nights we slept in our clothes and by daylight stood on the road watching big tanker planes and scooper helicopters pour fire retardant and gigantic buckets of water on the flames slowly creeping down Mulholland Highway just below our house. We went through our fire routine: Motor hooked up to the pool intake, garbage cans of water in the patio and plenty of gunnysacks ready. The wind changed. Once again we were spared.

Fire is not just a fact of life in Malibu. It is all over Southern California. New developments abound in marginal areas where the annual dry gale-force winds blow over water-starved vegetation. Houses are built closer and closer together. Just one spark and another disaster!

Even so, I can't consider a rainbow of springtime wildflowers and hillsides of blooming chaparral as mere "fuel for another big fire."

Chapter 8

MALIBU DISASTER

Rain can be as disastrous to Malibu as fire. In my years of living on the beach we experienced several really frightening storms with gigantic waves that left the sand 15 feet below the living room. With our beach house farther from the water than many, we lost nothing but sand. The rains of 1978 reminded my friend Betty Smith of the March 2, 1938 storm that took the Smith house on Las Flores Beach out to sea. This is what she told me:

"It had been raining for a week and I noticed the water was running across the highway from the canyon up in back of our house. I piled rocks against the house where this canyon drained into the ocean, but at 3 a.m. the whole house went bumping down toward the beach.

"Suddenly our bedroom opened to the whole outdoors. Our two girls, sleeping in a bunkroom in the center of the house, were okay, but what about our little boy? His room was up closer to the highway, a former garage that we had converted into sleeping quarters for him. The side of the house was gone. Water was knee deep everywhere. All of our trees had disappeared. The place looked like a landscape on Mars, plus that muddy water pouring all over. We couldn't even see the room where our son was. We were terrified. Had we had lost our little boy? We all started to walk to our neighbors, Florence and Fred Harrison, and suddenly we heard a small voice calling, 'M o t h e r! Come and get my mother! The house is gone!'

"That was the sweetest sound I've ever heard. It didn't matter that the whole house was gone and we had only the nightclothes we were standing in. Our little boy was safe!

"Then it seemed to be funny. The bathtub was standing up halfway down to the beach. The living room furniture had just disappeared."

Betty told me they and the Harrisons walked through the mud on the highway to the Las Flores Inn. Nobody answered their knock, so they forced their way into a house next to the Inn where they spent the rest of the night. By daylight they discovered both of their cars were lost, one right into the ocean, the other so deep in the sand, it was useless. But Betty remembered that in the melee not one dish in the kitchen was broken, and also that Malibu people were kind and helpful, just as they are today.

The "Smith Family Malibu" took a vote on whether to stay or leave. It was unanimous: "Stay." They proceeded to build a house out of the way of that draining canyon across the highway, at 21036 Pacific Coast Highway, right next door to their friends, the Harrisons. Betty and I sat on the deck of this same house and she reminisced about a Malibu I had yet to discover.

The Smiths came to California to live in 1928 after Horace (her late husband) had sold his automobile business in St.Louis. They first lived in Santa Monica, then in Pacific Palisades where they rented a five-bedroom house for $50 a month. This house was sold out from under them. That spring, 1932, they rented a place on the beach for six months to avoid the summer boost in rents.

They investigated property in Malibu and found a house on Las Flores Beach for sale for $800, which was cheaper than renting, "and if we don't like it at the beach, we can sell it," they told each other. They sat on the steps of the house and watched the full moon make its silvery path across the water. Betty said, "That clinched the deal."

The house was small, but it had a wide porch all across the front. Betty remembered they had spent $500 more and had part of the porch enclosed to make another room. The land under the house belonged to William Randolph Hearst, who leased it to them for $20 a month.

Betty remembered Pacific Coast Highway then in the early thirties as a nicely paved two-lane road. The Santa Monica school bus picked up the children and brought them home each day. Grocery shopping had to be done in Santa Monica, although people could buy bread and fish at the Las Flores Inn. At that time there were no electric refrigerators, but the iceman came out to Malibu twice a week and the milkman regularly delivered milk.

"The worst thing was the water." Betty told me. She said they paid a cent a gallon to have a truck come out "to fill our tank." (No water pipes yet.) The Smith house was all electric, but with no water heater. Betty described a copper kettle one of their friends built for them: "It fitted the stove burner exactly and we'd heat that full of water to boiling. My husband would carry it to the bathroom and dump the water into the tiny tub. Cold tap water made it the right temperature, but we didn't get a bath every day!"

Telephone service to Malibu was on a party line (still in effect in 1949). The Smiths heated their house with an electric floor furnace designed by Horace Smith, who at that time worked for the Ward Floor Furnace Company.

Betty told me that the Malibu fire of 1938 was just before Thanksgiving, when their new house was only sixs months old. She was in Santa Monica shopping. Someone recognized her car and left a note on the windshield telling her where to rendezvous with her husband, the Harrisons and all the children.

Word came to them that everything between Topanga and Las Flores had been destroyed. They were not permitted to go home for hours, and when they finally did drive home along the beach, they saw nearly total devastation. What a relief, as they rounded the last curve, to see their new home unharmed! That was a REAL Thanksgiving!

Las Flores Beach residents credited Messers. Grimshaw and Golding, owners of Las Flores Inn, with saving their homes. The two men went around with their spritz bottles and dowsed the sparks with soda water.

Betty had been a widow for several years at the time of my interview, years in which she had traveled all over the world, taking prize-winning photographs along the way. But she said to her the "prize winner" is this: and she showed me her photo of a view from her sun porch: a complete panorama of Santa Monica Bay. She said it was one of those "Maliblue Days." The view is from the same place that she and her husband sat and watched the moon over the water the time they decided to "try living in Malibu" all these nearly 50 years ago.

Chapter 9

DECKER SCHOOL

Like Marion Decker in California, my grandfather, James Danskin, homesteaded land in Iowa. Like Marion Decker's grandchildren, I, too attended a one-room country school in the 1920's. My father brought our family to California in 1923, when the Decker School was thriving. But, by 1949 when my husband and I came to live in Malibu, the school had practically served its purpose. I read with dismay about its end—razed to the ground on January 24, 1968. But it wasn't until 10 years later, when we lived just a quick walk from Decker Canyon Road that I began to put together the whole story.

Note: The Decker Dynasty: Marion Decker homesteader – 1885

His son: Charley M. Decker, wife Martha A.

His grandson: Charles M. Decker – son of Charley M.

His great-grandson: Charles Decker.

It really began in 1862 when the United States Congress passed the Homestead Act, which made public lands in the west available to settlers without payment, usually in parcels of 160 acres. The Rancho Malibu Topango Simi and Sequit extended only a mile inland from the Pacific and the Rancho Conejo came just to the base of the mountains on the east, so there were hundreds of acres of free public land available. Settlers began drifting in. Among them was Marion Decker, who claimed 160 acres in Aliso Canyon, about half way between the beginning of Rancho Malibu at Las Flores and the western end of the Ranch. He was the first of several Decker family members to homestead in the area, which became known as the Decker community.

Knowing of my interest in the history of this area, my neighbor, the late Jimmy Decker (a distant relative of Marion) gave me a copy of a certificate dated May 8, 1901, signed by President William McKinley, granting Charley M. Decker (Marion's son) 160 acres in what is now known as Decker Canyon.

As my research continued I discovered that the nearest school in this area was at Cornell, a small settlement several miles east of the Decker community. When that school closed in 1909 because there were not enough children it meant no school for Charley M. Decker's daughter, Helen. So her mother, Martha A. Decker, talked the neighboring Glenn Brothers, who raised racehorses nearby, into loaning her a tiny cabin on sled runners. She saw it as just big enough for a schoolroom for her daughter, two other little girls and their teacher, Mary Mohn. And that's how Decker School began.

It must have been sometime in the 1980's when I listened to a Malibu Historical Society taped interview with the late Helen Decker Marine and learned she was the little girl of the "sled-runner" cabin and the first Decker school. She told how she and her schoolmates watched it being pulled out into the sunshine on cool days and back into the shade when

his is Malibu Colony Beach in 1926 when Mae Rindge gave Warner Bros. the first permit
› film a movie on her Rancho Malibu. Here is a scene from "On the Pacific" - the story of a
hilippine insurrection. Artificial palm trees transform the uninhabited Malibu Colony Beach
ıto a tropical setting for the U.S. Army camp, complete with tents and marching soldiers.
?hoto: Permission of Warner Bros.)

The Whole Class. The teacher is on the porch of Ed Campbell's summer hunting cabin. It was Decker School from 1911 until 1919. (Malibu Historical Society Photo)

Off to Decker school. Students and their burros ready to take the 3 ½ mile trail ride up and over the mountain in 1918 or 1919. (Kathleen Parks Goebel Photo)

In 1923 Decker students pose in front of school and the new volleyball net. (Kathleen Parks Goebel Photo)

It's a "Full House" and in 1955 Decker School closed. Students were bused to the new Juan Cabrillo School in Malibu. (Malibu Historical Society Photo)

Driving "The Track" from Santa Monica to the Las Flores gates of Rancho Malibu in 1911. Ten years later it was paved with cement slabs. (California Dept. of Highways Photo)

Trestle spanning Ramirez Canyon for the Malibu Ranch's railroad, early 1900's (Malibu Historical Society Photo)

FIND GOLD NEAR L. A.

TREASURE HIDDEN IN SANTA MONICA HILLS

She's In Spotlight Today
Mrs. Delmont On Stand

Los Angeles Record

2 CENTS 5 O'CLOCK EDITION

FATTY AGAIN IN COURT

DRINK CAUSES DUAL TRAGEDY

SEMNACHER TO TELL

ONE MAN INJURED

CONVICTS

7 CAPTURED IN RAID ON DOPE

BOOKS

HANG OUT OLD GLORY

Los Angeles Record on September 21, 1911 tells of gold discovery in Malibu (Santa Monica Evening Outlook Photo).

ne of the last remaining steel balls from incaid's mill that pulverized the rocks, aving gold dust as residue. (Santa Monica ening Outlook Photo)

Evelyn and Joe show me the opening of the mine on a steep poison-oak-covered hillside. (Santa Monica Evening Outlook Photo)

The oil well on Point Dume in 1924. Note the Malibu Ranch Zuma Canyon barn (left-center background). (UCLA department of Geography Air Photo archives)

Foundation work on Malibu Dam in 1924 (Photo Courtesy of Malibu Lagoon Museum).

The Dam overflows. (Photo Courtesy of Malibu Lagoon Museum)

Malibu Creek in flood above the Dam (Undated photo from Malibu Lagoon Museum)

Malibu Dam much as it looks now. (Malibu Lagoon Museum Photo)

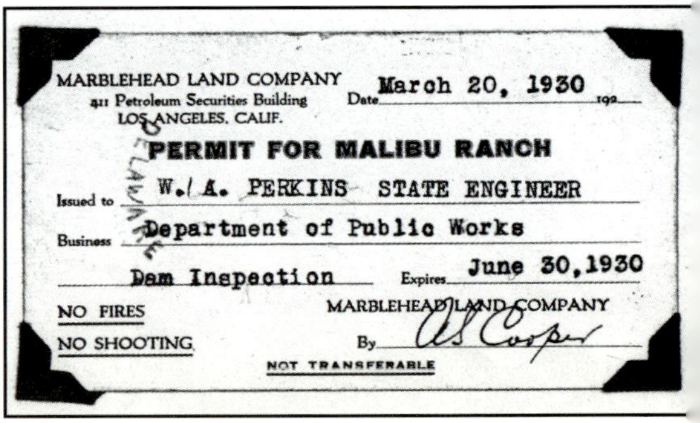

MARBLEHEAD LAND COMPANY
411 Petroleum Securities Building
LOS ANGELES, CALIF.

Date March 20, 1930 192

PERMIT FOR MALIBU RANCH

Issued to W./ A. PERKINS STATE ENGINEER

Business Department of Public Works

Dam Inspection Expires June 30,1930

NO FIRES

NO SHOOTING

MARBLEHEAD LAND COMPANY

By A S Cooper

NOT TRANSFERABLE

Permission to inspect the dam, 1930.
(Malibu Lagoon Museum)

Malibu Creek Bridge is widened in 1949.
(California Department of Highways Photo).

Pacific Coast Highway gets a new look, 1940. Bulldozers at work above Coral Canyon. (State of California Department of Highways Photo)

View of Malibu Colony Beach when PCH still was "Malibu Road". (Malibu Lagoon Museum Photo.

Peaceful morning on the Roberts Ranch in Solstice Canyon probably in the late 1940's (Private photo collection)

And here is the square dance after a Play Days pot luck supper. (Ralph Goodson Photo).

We're in position for a publicity shot to advertise "Malibu Play Days" (Lori Babbitt photo)

Malibu Riders Club barbecue (Ralph Goodson Photo).

"All Aboard" for a ride on the fire engine—Malibu Play Days (Ralph Goodson Photo).

My angel from "The Angel Factory" about 1960.
(Private collection)

the weather was hot. She didn't say how many years the school continued in this rustic building. Nor did she tell the exact location of it.

Her brother, Charles M. Decker (son of Charley M. Decker), told me the little school on sled runners was "at the bottom of La Chusa Canyon on the Glenn Ranch." He said he was only three or four years old at the time, and did not remember if the school was in continuous use.

In 1911, probably about the beginning of the school year in September Ed Campbell, one of the neighbors, converted his summer hunting cabin into a schoolhouse.

The Decker School District (named in honor of Charles M. Decker's father, Marion, who homesteaded in Encinal Canyon in 1885) was officially formed on January 29, 1912. The Malibu Mountain areas of Los Angeles County (north of the western end of Rancho Topango Malibu Simi and Sequit) were in the Liberty School District, which also included Calabasas and Las Virgenes.

My interest really grew when, in Los Angeles County records, I found Mary B. Shirley listed as Decker School principal in 1912. Average daily attendance that year was eight students. The district was suspended August 7, 1913, but at Martha Decker's insistence it was immediately reinstated with Margaret J. E. Brown as principal. Mrs. Decker even took in "county children" to live with the family to go to school just to keep it open.

One day our neighbor, Jimmy Decker, in conversation happened to mention that Pepperdine Professor James Wilburn's grandmother taught at Decker School in the early days. My reportorial instinct was really aroused. Professor Wilburn put me in touch with his aunt, Alice Wilburn Clevenger Gable.

In letters and telephone conversations, Alice Gable described life at Decker School in 1914—1915, the year she was in the third grade and her mother was the teacher.

Alice remembers riding in Mr. (Charley M.) Decker's wagon up into the hills from the Russell ranch on Ventura Highway. "Near the end of the eight-mile drive we passed the red shed-like school just before coming over a rise and got our first view of the Decker home."

Earlier that summer, Alice's mother, Harriet Wilburn, had made the tedious journey to the Decker home from Los Angeles. She took the Pacific Electric streetcar to the end of the line at Sherman Way and Owensmouth, in Canoga Park. Then she boarded the Wells Fargo Ventura bus to the Russell ranch (the present Westlake Village). There Charley M. Decker met her with his horse drawn wagon and they drove up and over the hills.

Mrs. Wilburn met the Decker family and signed a contract to teach at Decker School for a year. The next day she returned to Los Angeles to get her family ready for the move. She agreed to bring the four youngest of her six children with her to keep up the attendance so the school could stay open.

During the 1914-1915 school year, Decker School's total enrollment consisted of: Kitty, Trixie, Pearl, Charles M., and Helen Decker; and Alice, Dorothy, Jim, and Mark Wilburn.

Mrs. Gable described the 1914 "teacherage" as a "two-room cabin": the kitchen, furnished with a dining table, benches, storage shelves and a wood stove that provided cooking facilities and was the only heating source; the second room, which boasted two double beds, a cot, a chest or two, and "Mama's ever-present trunk." Canvas roll-ups covered the open-to-the-world windows instead of glass. These were pulled up or let down according to the weather. "We carried water from the stream nearby."

I was reminded that in 1914, Decker Canyon Road, Mulholland and Pacific Coast Highway did not exist. School desks and all supplies had to be brought up the eight-mile wagon track from Ventura Highway either on the backs of mules or horses, or in Charley M. Decker's wagon.

Life in Decker Canyon involved the entire Wilburn family. On Saturday, Brother Mark walked the seven-mile trail to Cornell with the weekly grocery order and picked up the groceries, leaving the order for the next week. He also brought back the weekly mail. He carried the heavy bags on his back until the family got a burro. Mark and brother Jim, Professor Wilburn's father, chopped all of the wood for the cook stove and Alice and Dorothy helped their mother with the cleaning, washing and baking on Saturdays.

Alice remembered, rather than carry all the water up the hill from the creek to the cabin, "We arranged washing and bathing facilities beside the stream, weather permitting." In vacation times, the family walked the eight miles to Ventura Highway to catch the bus for their trek to Los Angeles. Alice remembered she was grateful for the rest stops.

Charles M. Decker, (grandson of Marion Decker and son of Charley M. Decker) entered school in the little hunting cabin the fall of 1913 and continued until just before his graduation from the eighth grade. He went to Santa Monica to live with one of his sisters and finished grammar school there. He put me in touch with his schoolmate, Kathleen Parks, who continued my Decker School story with her reminiscences:

Kathleen's father, jeweler Eugene Parks of Venice, California, came out into the country for his health. He took up the homestead of one of his friends in Sequit Canyon (at the far western border of the Malibu Rancho). The original home place was on the Yerba Buena (Ventura County) side of the property, so Kathleen attended the Yerba Buena School. But there was a better home site on the east side of the property, and the family built a new house there, (close to the site of the present-day Camp for the Junior Blind). This was in the Decker District, so Kathleen entered the fifth grade at Decker School – three and one-half miles up and over the mountains.

She had become Kathleen Parks Goebel when she talked to me in her Thousand Oaks home. She told me her first teacher at Decker School had two pre-school age children who were "always under foot" and that the school board asked her to leave at midterm. Kathleen did not remember the name of the unfortunate lady, and I did not find it in Los Angeles County records. But I did discover Delphina Fowler taught Decker School in 1918, the last term in the little summer hunting cabin.

On January 29, 1919, Charley M. Decker and his wife, Martha A. Decker, gave a grant deed to the Decker School District of Los Angeles County for a one-acre parcel of land "to be used for school purposes." And at the same time Martha "floated a bond issue to have a new school built that would include a library and lodging for the teacher." Their son, Charles M. (confusingly named after his father) told me. The neat clapboard building was completed in 1919 in time for the opening of the fall term in September with Mary L. Sterrett as the new teacher.

Kathleen said she enjoyed her studies in the new Decker School building. She remembered, one day when Mrs. Sterrett was teaching she stopped in mid-sentence as she looked toward the door, turned pale, held onto her desk and sat down. "We kids all turned around and, there in the doorway, in his U.S. Army uniform, stood our teacher's son, Jack, home from the war. Needless to say, school was dismissed for a week!"

Kathleen remembered she had to get up at five a.m. every morning to milk the goats and cows. Her father surveyed and widened the trail so she and the "county children" who lived with the family, could ride burros or horses those three-and-one-half miles to school instead of trudging through the chaparral on foot. Kathleen went to live with an aunt in Roseville, California, and graduated from the eighth grade there. Then she stayed home for a year. For the 1922-23 terms, Decker School added the first two years of high school, so Kathleen returned.

That year Ernest H. Horton taught grades four through seven and both nine and ten. For Kathleen, ninth grade subjects were English, Spanish, ancient history and algebra. Tenth grade studies included more English and Spanish, plus English history and geometry. (This was the first and only time 10th grade subjects were offered in Malibu until Colin McEwen High School opened in 1980. Malibu High School was dedicated in 1992).

Teachers changed each year at Decker School, with Gertrude Helena Blanchard on the records for 1924 and Mrs. Dorothea T. Hoover for 1925. But in September 1926 Mrs. Helena Kelly Weaver came to Decker School with her two children, Betty and Ben. She remained the Decker School's "principal and janitor" (according to county records) for 30 years, until the school was closed in 1955.

Average daily attendance at Decker School in 1926 was 10 students.

That was the year the Mason family came out to live on their Mulholland ranch and Richard Mason entered Decker School. Florence and Atha Decker and their three boys, Earl, James and Clyde, had migrated to California from Baton Rouge, Louisiana, and settled in Los Alisos Canyon that year, too, adding more children to the Decker School roll. All three boys graduated under Mrs. Weaver's guidance: Earl in 1931, James, "Jimmy", in 1932, and Clyde in 1937.

Decker School pupils had to find their own way to school until 1939, when bus service finally began. There must have been a regular stable on the school grounds, as many of the kids rode horses, including Kathleen Parks.

Twice in Mrs. Weaver's 30 years at the school, fire came close. The October 30, 1930 fire stopped before it reached the school building, but the second one, October 23, 1935 was "the most exciting event" in her life, Mrs. Weaver remembered.

She told an *Outlook* reporter the school children spotted the puff of smoke in the northeast during the morning recess and how that puff of smoke "expanded until a huge black cloud spread over the sky and began to approach very fast." Parents arrived to help, and so did a road crew working nearby. Men climbed onto the roof and doused it with water while the mothers and Mrs. Weaver readied wet towels. The danger passed and the school was saved, but several nearby homes were destroyed. The school was turned into the refuge for the families who had no place to go.

The Santa Monica newspaper reported fears for the safety of the 15 children at Decker School in this devastating fire that claimed, among countless others, the Zuma Canyon headquarters of the Rindge ranch.

As always, life went on, and over the years Decker School became more and more the community center for families living in and around Decker Canyon. There were potluck suppers, box socials and dances, as well as Sunday school, even though religious activities were not a part of Los Angeles County's regular school program.

In the late 1930's the second generation of Decker students arrived at school: Helen Decker Marine's daughter, Helen; Charles M. Decker's sons Charles (continuing the family tradition naming), and Jack; Earl Decker's son, Bert. By the 1950's there was a third generation Decker student: Cheri Marron, daughter of Helen Marine Marron.

Mrs. Weaver told a newspaper reporter, "Over the years, since I first began teaching, there has been a decided change in teaching practices. In the past it seemed to me more attention was given to teaching the fundamentals and not so much to the social activities and physical education. There were not as many subjects to be taught and the program was not as flexible as at the present time. In this type of school with only one teacher and eight grades, it has been necessary to stick to a pretty rigid schedule.

"Under the Los Angeles County School System," Mrs. Weaver added, "Decker School enjoyed the facilities of the Los Angeles library and had help in art, music, physical education, child guidance, speech correction, health problems, and audio-visual education."

After World War II when Rancho Topango Malibu Simi and Sequit land went on the market people began to come to live in the Trancas and Broad Beach areas, all in the Decker School District. By 1949 Decker School had 26 pupils – 20 from along Pacific Coast Highway and six from the Canyon. Sometime between 1949 and 1951 the Decker District purchased land on Zuma Mesa for a new school.

County records show two boys and two girls graduated from the eighth grade in 1949. One girl graduated in 1951. By then most seventh graders who lived along the highway took the bus to junior high in Santa Monica.

On November 12, 1951, a committee from Decker School District, composed of Mrs. Emrich Nicolson, Mrs. Edna King, Pete Garcia and Floyd Ferguson, met with the Santa Monica School Board to explore the possibility of joining the Santa Monica School District.

The 26 pupils presently enrolled crowded the one room school practically to the limit. With more and more people coming to live within the district, an enrollment of 50 was predicted in the foreseeable future.

The new people in the district came from cities where there was but one grade per classroom, with a teacher for each. They felt their children needed the advantages of a more modern school and were willing to have them ride buses.

The Santa Monica Board voted to accept the Decker District if the people wished to come into the Santa Monica District; to build a new school on the Decker District's Zuma Mesa land; to earmark money received from the State for Decker to be used to meet financial needs in building and operation.

The board agreed to maintain the present school until a new school could be built; to provide adequate transportation comparable to that of the present time for the Decker District; and to retain the present teacher of the Decker District.

More than half of the registered voters in the district signed the petition to join Santa Monica and the County Superintendent of Schools presented it to the Board of Supervisors on Tuesday, November 25, 1952.

The supervisors granted the request, and Decker School District was consolidated into the Santa Monica District. This action was not unanimously accepted by the Decker Canyon Community. From pioneer days they had retained their independence, and wished to handle their school in their own way. The poll taken July 31, 1952 showed 57 people in favor of joining the Santa Monica District and 87 opposing the move. The vote changed in favor of the consolidation when unregistered voters were removed from the list.

The original petition was on file (1984) in the Office of School Organization and Elections.

Twenty square miles, formerly in the Decker District, were added to the Santa Monica Unified School District when the consolidation went into effect in July, 1953. That year Decker School's daily attendance was 19.

The new school, Juan Cabrillo, was built on the former Decker District's property on Zuma Mesa. Decker School closed at the end of the school year, June 3, 1955. Juan Cabrillo opened in September 1955, with Mrs. Weaver as fourth grade teacher. She retired at the end of the school year in June, 1956, after 30 years of teaching.

But what about the Decker schoolhouse? It stood empty until 1968, when on January 24 the Santa Monica Unified School District had it razed to the ground.

Plans to use the site for a reconstructed Chumash village where third graders could study the Indian tribe that once inhabited Malibu never happened, and 16 years later—in 1984—when I went to look at the site, I found that the chain-link fence still encircled the empty grounds. The maypole still stood, minus its ropes. The water tank had vanished but the well house remained. The teacher's corrugated iron garage was filled with a scattering of debris ranging from a wall shelf and broken chair to a moldering book.

Enough of the concrete foundation remained so I could find the outlines of the school building beside the weed-grown blacktop remains of the playground. I was surprised to see the basketball standards still standing upright, with their backboards fallen to the ground. An aged Pontiac occupied the bus garage.

At that time the acre of ground remained the property of the Santa Monica Unified District. Rory Livingston was in charge of evaluating all of the district's property.

I remembered that back in 1919 Charley M. and Martha A. Decker had specified in their grant deed to this property that it be used "solely and exclusively for school purposes, and in the event that said property shall not be used, it shall revert to and be vested in said grantors."

The day Decker School was demolished, Helen Decker Marine told a reporter she feared the school's cornerstone had been "carried off by the wreckers." A teacher told the reporter, "The stone has been put aside and probably will be set in cement to commemorate the school."

But in 1989 I found the Decker School cornerstone in cement at the corner of Kanan-Dume Road and Pacific Coast Highway along with a time capsule to commemorate the opening of the Malibu-Kanan Center.

And now as I write (2004) the cornerstone is gone; demolished when the newest owners expanded their building. The contents have been returned to the people whose addresses were in the metal box inside the cement.

As for the Decker School acre – the heirs did not reclaim the school property after the Santa Monica School District abandoned it. Eventually it was sold and neighbors are in the process of negotiations to build a road alongside the acre from Decker School Road into the area where Marion Decker had built his adobe home 100 years ago.

Chapter 10

LIBRARIES

The other day errands took me to the Heathercliff shopping area. I was surprised to see the Los Angeles County Library's Bookmobile parked there near the market. It brought back memories of Malibu in the 1950's when Bookmobile day was the occasion to meet our friends and exchange greetings as well as books.

How did the Bookmobile happen? Los Angeles County's population increased astronomically after World War II and the central library was hard put to keep up with the need for new facilities to serve all of the outlying communities. The Antelope Valley with a burgeoning population was the farthest from the central library. One day someone came up with the idea of a mobile library as a stopgap to putting up more buildings. Beginning in 1949 the first "Bookmobile" made 45 stops each week throughout the entire Antelope Valley. Malibu was next on the list and got its Bookmobile that same year.

The Bookmobile was a godsend for us doing research 20 years before we had the Malibu Civic Center and our own library. If anyone wanted a reference book, books for the children or even a "good read," we patronized the Bookmobile. It made 22 regular stops each week within the area from Calabasas and Topanga Canyon to Trancas, including six locations along the length of Malibu.

"Our" Bookmobile was stocked and sent out from the Lennox Branch of the Los Angeles County Public Library in West Hollywood. The first librarian and driver had to negotiate steep, winding mountain roads and devious surface streets. Travel had become a bit easier by 1960 when Mrs. Ruth George and her driver, Tony, manned the Bookmobile.

Bookmobile stopping places were to Malibu what the village fountain was in Old Spanish pueblos – the place where we gals exchanged news and the children met their friends. In addition we found new books to read. The Bookmobile always had something interesting for the grown-ups or new picture books and stories for the children. The entire Los Angeles County Library's stock was available to us – we had only to put in our request. The book usually would be on the Bookmobile the next week. Mrs. George and Tony had so many friends at each stop often someone would bring them sandwiches and coffee or soft drinks.

Alanna Niles remembers one hectic day when one of her friends had missed the La Costa stop by a minute. She got into her car and flagged down the Bookmobile enroute to Big Rock. Tony stopped and the lady turned in her due books. (When PCH traffic was not yet formidable.) Then I discovered there was a branch of the Los Angeles County Library in the Malibu area long before the Bookmobile was invented.

It all began back in 1912. The first Los Angeles County Library headquarters took up just two "unfurnished rooms on the top floor of the 'new' Hall of Records" writes Roger H. Woelfel in his book commemorating the library's 75th anniversary in 1987.

The first branch library in what was to become the county's library system was established April 23, 1913 in the Willowbrook home of Mrs. Belle B. Jenks, who served as "custodian." She had no reading room in her house, but put up a shelf for the 50 books to be put in circulation. Almost immediately there were 63 registered borrowers who came during the four hours a week the library was open.

Right away requests came in for other branches. These were established in the order in which they were received – 18 granted by June of 1913. Our Decker community was one of the first.

In 1913 there was no road through the Rancho Malibu. The only entrance to the Decker area was up and over the mountains from the San Fernando Valley. Library books were packed over the trail on horse- or mule-back. A shelf in the schoolroom held the books, with the teacher as custodian.

The new 1919 Decker School had a" branch library room," according to reminiscences of the late Helen Decker Marine in the Malibu Historical Society archives. Mrs. Marine had been a pupil in Decker School when it was a temporary building on sled runners.

My neighbor, the late Florence Decker, told me she was the first Los Angeles County librarian at the school, starting in 1930. She said library days were Mondays and Fridays and the library was patronized by practically all of the Decker area residents and some even farther away. She described the room as small, "but with a beautiful view down the canyon to the ocean." Decker School had the only county free lending library in what is now the Malibu area for the next 19 years, when the Bookmobile was organized.

After Leota Elliott established her "Little Store" in the Malibu La Costa area, she installed a very small rental library of popular fiction with the emphasis on "whodunits." But for reference and general reading we all patronized the Bookmobile.

May 27, 1968 was "Groundbreaking Day" for the Malibu Civic Center. Construction began in June, with completion scheduled for 1969. Soon after that Malibu had its own spacious County library.

That marked the end of the Bookmobile's stop at the Mayfair Market. We felt in the "lap of luxury" with the new library – spacious reading room, lines of card files, places for the children to choose their own books – really nice! Then came "Prop 13" – the referendum that drastically reduced property taxes. In their wisdom, the county supervisors cut funding for libraries and music education in the schools. When we voted the "prop" in, we visualized cutting the unnecessary bureaucracy, not cultural activities. We were appalled.

This being Malibu, Margaret Richardson, who had been a member of the Pacific Palisades chapter, got in touch with the "Friends of the Library" and established a chapter here with the assistance of Bill and Rosemary Hoppe. When the library hours were cut down to two days a week, the Friends provided funds to open it one more day. Today the Friends' main fundraising activity is an annual book fair to provide money for "extras" for the library.

When county funding resumed, the Malibu library added several computers and another "online" for the use of library cardholders. The Malibu library (in 2004) is a "C" library – graded on total circulation – and is at the end of the line for county funding. If we want to rate "B" or "A" more people must become patrons. The children's' section has expanded with many innovative programs for youngsters, especially in summertime.

The Bookmobile came back to Heathercliff after a small branch of the County library closed when the Marine Science School on Point Dume opened. The hours are every Tuesday from 10 a.m. to noon and from 1:30 p.m. to 4:00 p.m. The day I visited Bookmobile, assistant librarian and driver was Mahnoosh Maleki with Craig Talbott as her aide. She told me there were 2,000 volumes on the neatly arranged shelves and that the circulation is 200.

As I browsed through the shelves I couldn't help but notice how different this Bookmobile is from the one I knew in 1949. There now are books on tape, videos and CDs – unheard of 50 years ago. But the same courtesy applies now as then: "If it isn't on the Bookmobile, our registrants may request anything that is in the Los Angeles County library system." A special shelf filled with books wrapped in the library request forms attests to the popularity of this convenient service. Some things have not changed with time.

Chapter 11

MALIBU DAM

Of the thousands of motorists who travel up and down Malibu Canyon Road every day, perhaps just one realizes that Malibu Dam spans the creek below. It's nearly three miles up the canyon from the ocean and is visible from a couple of the lookouts along the Canyon Road.

When my husband and I first came to Malibu more than 50 years ago one of the "sights" was to see Malibu Creek pouring over the dam in a big rainstorm. We would drive up to the Honor Camp lookout (years before Malibu Canyon Road was built) and watch the rust-color spray as water cascaded over the dam. In a really bad storm the spray would be hundreds of feet in the air.

Once upon a time steelhead trout may have made their way from the Pacific Ocean up Malibu Creek to complete their life cycle and spawn in the Creek's headwaters somewhere in the western edge of San Fernando Valley. This "time" has sparked a three-decade controversy over the pros and cons of removing Malibu Dam.

May K. Rindge built the dam to irrigate her alfalfa fields and vegetable gardens. Her grandson, Ronald, believes any steelhead trout above the dam at any time to be apocryphal. He showed me photos of a waterfall that flowed over the rocks upon which the dam was built and says that no trout could surmount it. Rather than destroy the dam, he would like to see it desilted and remain as a precious reservoir for fighting Malibu fires.

On the other hand California Trout maintains that before the dam was built (in 1924) an estimated population of 1,000 steelhead trout spawned in the Malibu Creek watershed. California Trout has provided enough evidence to secure the Southern Steelhead Trout as a federally endangered species. That means "NO FISHING" wherever these fish are.

In 2003 a $2 million grant had the Army Corps of Engineers at work on a feasibility study to determine what should be done with the dam - remove it completely, or remove it by degrees over the course of 20 or so years in the hope that eventually the trout will return to their old habitat upstream. This is the situation regarding the dam as this chapter of Malibu life is being written.

The idea for a story about the Malibu Dam came to me after I had joined an early spring morning hike up Malibu Creek with a group of Malibu Lagoon Museum docents. A huge rainstorm a few days before had filled the creek. We intended to get to the foot of the dam, about a two-mile hike. It was rough going, pushing through the flood debris and either going around or climbing over some large twisted rusty steel pipes. Our way was completely blocked after less than a mile.... just enough to whet my appetite to find out more about the dam.

So a few weeks later, with the assistance of Malibu Creek State Park Ranger Randy Sederquist in his trusty four-wheel-drive jeep and with photographer Tom Dobyns, I set out to see the dam from the bottom up. Surprise! Not more than a block down the steep track from Malibu Canyon Road the jeep trail was washed out, leaving only a horse trail. We abandoned the jeep and slogged along for an hour until that trail, too disappeared. After another hour of strenuous boulder bashing and sliding on mid-stream slippery rocks, we called it a day without seeing the dam!

It was a shame to give up, but the cameraman had fallen into the creek (but kept his camera dry) and we had brought neither food nor water. We were "bushed" and turned around and slogged the two miles back to the jeep.

Beautiful scenery compensated for the hard walking. Long, quiet pools reflected the blue sky. Tall rushes and small bright flowers lived at the stream's edge. Myriads of tiny fish flashed in backwater puddles we waded through. Birds sang in the willows. The sandy banks showed raccoon tracks and we saw signs of fox. We passed a couple of optimistic anglers casting their lines in one of the larger pools.

I knew that years ago people who had property in Serra Canyon received irrigation water from the Malibu Dam, but I needed to go back to where it started. Through the help of the Division of Safety of Dams in Sacramento along with photographs from the archives of the Malibu Lagoon Museum, this is what I found:

The 80-year-old dam is located in Malibu Creek about three miles up Malibu Canyon from the beach. It is visible from several "View Sites" on Malibu Canyon Road. Now it impounds no water - just the Malibu Creek run-off from the Tapia wastewater plant trickling through the sand, rocks, and brush and over the tons of silt where once there had been a reservoir.

At 100 feet, the Malibu Dam is the highest of the four dams built over the years on Malibu Creek and its tributaries. First of these, called "Rocky Pass Reservoir" was built in 1904 by F. W. Mathiesen. It was built to impound Lake Sherwood in Ventura County. The "Craggs Country Club" dam, built in 1913, provided a small lake for the Club.

Malibou Lake Club's dam, built in 1923, is 50 feet high with a 120-foot spillway and impounds 1000 acre-feet of water. Malibu Dam impounded 575 acre-feet of water to irrigate the Marblehead Land Company's alfalfa fields below the dam.

In 1924 it was not necessary to have a permit to build a dam, but frequent inspections by state engineers were required. First of these at Malibu was March 27 of that year. Consulting Engineer A.M. Strong, employed by Marblehead Land Company, May K. Rindge, president, had inquired about the permit procedure. By that time a wagon road leading to the dam site was ready and initial preparation for the foundation was in progress.

Actual concrete pouring for May Rindge's dam began early in August of 1924. The dread foot and mouth disease epidemic raged throughout California's cattle herds and strict quarantine regulations made it difficult to add workmen to the small force of the Ranch's day laborers, used for the preliminary work. The August inspection of the dam's foundation, which went 20 feet below bedrock, was declared satisfactory and work on the dam continued.

I would like to have seen the two "high wires" that were strung 130 feet above Malibu Creek's streambed with the buckets of concrete swinging to where they were emptied. They were filled with "Condor" cement from Belgium mixed with sand from the creek in a "two-yard" mixer. The concrete then was transferred to the buckets for pouring. The dam was built to last. It is reinforced with 60-pound rails from Rancho Malibu's abandoned "Malibu and Port Hueneme Railroad."

Inspectors questioned the quality of the low-priced Belgium cement. But extensive laboratory tests proved it to be slow setting, and otherwise not inferior to American brands. Using another type of sand and gravel right from the creek bed easily solved initial problems with some aggregate. The inspectors warned the construction engineers to be certain that the concrete around the horizontal rails was thoroughly tamped in for maximum strength. By December of 1924, when the arch of the dam was completed, it contained 30,000 sacks of cement equaling 4000 yards of concrete at a cost of $65,000. (Compare that to what it might cost now).

To illustrate some of the "equivalents": Deputy Engineer E.C. Eaton presented a bill to Marblehead on January 6,1925 for $4.96 auto expense for 62 miles at 8 cents per mile. Another bill requested:

E.C. Eaton, 1 day @ $350 per month - $11.29

Stenographer, 1 day @ $130 per month - $4.19

Expense, Eaton - $11.85

Auto, 206 mi. @ 8 cents per mile - $16.48

Total: $43.81

At this time Mrs. Rindge was so deeply involved in her lawsuit to keep the highway off the Malibu Ranch she was unable to finish the spillway. All of the engineers recommended this be completed for safety in case of a flood that would send more than five feet of water over the top of the dam.

But the winter of 1924-25 brought no floods and by May of 1925 preparations for the spillway were well under way. Wayne Loel, the geologist and consulting engineer who had built the dam, promised the spillway would be concreted before the 1926 flood season. That did not happen.

By September of 1925 Loel reported to the State Engineer he was "having some difficulties with the Rindge people" up to the point that when he was away from the job, his office was broken into and everything was taken out - including all of his field drawings for the entire work.

May Rindge engaged another engineer, Harry Hawgood, and a year later, after another flood season, the spillway was completed in September 1926. For this project workmen had moved 8000 cubic yards of dirt and rocks and covered the spillway with 2000 cubic yards of concrete at a cost of about $80,000, which included the price of the radial gates $3,000 F.O.B. job.

In June of 1928 Loel's suit against the Marblehead Land Company was still pending.

The July 1929 inspection of the dam showed that during one of the heavy floods (possibly the one in 1927 when the Las Turas Dam (Lake Sherwood) upstream gave way and sent 15 feet of water cascading over the top of Malibu Dam and down the spillway) there had been damage to the soft rock backing of the spillway. Deputy State Engineer W.A. Perkins suggested the area be refilled, drained, and surfaced with concrete and that the other side of the dam be grouted to prevent further damage. He noted also that the dam's final plans had never been given to the state office and told the State Engineer that "now there is unfriendly feeling" between Marblehead Land Company and Engineer Hawgood as well as Loel and Strong.

Locked gates greeted the deputy state engineers when they went for their regular inspection of Malibu Dam in February 1930. After telephone conversations with the Marblehead manager, another trip to the ranch and a process of rounding up someone to open the gate, the inspectors completed their job two days later.

In his letter to Mrs. Rindge, State Engineer George Hawley quoted in full the "Rules and Regulations and the Law Relative to Dam Supervision by the State Engineer" complete with the penalties for the violation thereof. He also enclosed an application blank for state approval of the dam.

A "Permit for the Malibu Ranch" was issued to W.A. Perkins, State Engineer, and Department of public works, on March 20, 1930 — to expire June 30, 1930. Another letter to Hawley in November 1930 signed by "M.K.Rindge" stated "The office of the Marblehead Land Company is to be notified when an Engineer wishes to make an inspection"and lists the six engineers authorized to use the permit - "to expire December 31, 1930." In return the engineers asked if a key to the gate could be kept in Marblehead's Los Angeles office so they could pick it up on their way out to the dam, and not have to depend on ranch personnel to open the gate.

Mrs. Rindge explained in another letter, "It is not our intention to hinder you in your duties of inspection of the Malibu Dam but it is our intention to use our best efforts to protect our interests and the large investments we have here in this canyon.

"Many curious persons try to obtain admission on various pretexts to our home place. Some succeed in gaining entrance, much to our annoyance, and we were therefore compelled to place a watchman at the gate with instructions to admit only those persons who have business on the property." She assured them of every courtesy, and enclosed eight passes. She added, "Locks on the gates may be changed at any time and it is not practical to issue keys."

May Rindge's attitude is understandable. The highway was open through the ranch, and after all of the publicity concerning the lengthy lawsuit against the state, people naturally were curious. In addition, her half-completed home for her family, "Rindge Castle," on a hill visible from the highway, was a magnet for "sightseers." The Malibu ranch still was private property.

No repairs were made to Malibu Dam for two more years. In August of 1932 the State Engineer issued an official order that the work was to be commenced before October and finished by December 31 of 1932. The Marblehead Land Company engaged a third engineer to work on the dam.

R.P. Webb of the Engineering Service Corporation had his crew start to clear out the brush and debris so he could see what needed to be done. Mrs. Rindge sent the State Engineer a list of the work to be accomplished (essentially the same as the state office had requested).

By December 23 the work was finished, with the exception of some grouting on the downstream side of the west abutment, which Mrs. Rindge deemed unessential. Deputy Engineer Holmes proposed the state issue a certificate of approval and order additional work as necessary, adding some specific conditions for the safe operation of the four radial gates on the spillway. Holmes also mentioned in a separate note that Engineer Webb wanted a statement from the State Engineer that the work on the dam had been completed so that he could collect from Marblehead.

Further inspection showed the questioned abutment all right under waterload and an "Order Authorizing Use of the Dam" was issued February 1, 1933 - nine years after it was completed.

After a 1935 inspection showed no increase in the seepage, Engineer Holmes recommended a certificate of approval for Malibu Dam. He noted, however, the radial gates to the spillway had not been made safe as requested in 1932. In 1931 Holmes had left a note for the Malibu ranch Superintendent Von Tol, stating the required chains had not been installed. At the 1935 inspection a Mr. Clark, the new man in charge of the water distribution system for the Malibu ranch, accompanied Holmes. He had seen the chains in the warehouse, and now that he knew what they were to be used for, would personally see they were put in place.

When contacted by telephone later that day Von Tol told Holmes the Malibu Ranch had gone into the hands of the receivers and he could not spend any money, but if the chains were available he, too, would see they were installed.

Eleven years after the start of the dam a certificate of approval was issued, dated October 15, 1935. State Engineer Hawley suggested the dam be regularly inspected three or four times each year and that in particular the progress of erosion or disintegration of the rock below the dam be noted.

After Marblehead Land Company sold the Rindge property in Serra Canyon, the land continued to benefit from irrigation water from the dam well into the 1940's. Dr. I W. Alexander's lemon grove, Ray Gagnon's property, Rhoda Adamson's vegetable garden, Walter Gunn's avocado orchard, Pete Kling's ranch, Jack Hazard's ranch, and the Serra Retreat gardens, all received water from the dam.

Late in 1953 Harry McDowell conceived the idea of an asphalt plant behind Malibu Dam. He proposed to dredge the silt from behind the dam in the manufacture of this material and applied to Los Angeles County for a permit. The Marblehead Land Company and the Malibu Water Company welcomed the asphalt plant as an inexpensive method of getting a dredging operation completed in Malibu's only sizeable water storage area.

The hearing before the Los Angeles County Regional Planning Commission took place on November 23, 1953. Unexpected opposition developed in the community on the grounds that an increase in truck traffic on recently completed Malibu Canyon Road would be too much of a hazard. (There had been several accidents at the original abrupt ending of the canyon road onto Pacific Coast Highway and parents of children in Webster School were concerned about heavy truck traffic on the road at the entrance to the school).

On December 11, 1953 the Regional Planning Commission granted a permit for a gravel-crushing plant in Malibu Canyon but vetoed the construction of an asphalt plant at the same location. McDowell protested the ruling at the next meeting of the planning commission, to no avail. Plans for the gravel-crushing operation were dropped and sand and silt continued to pile up behind the dam.

Fourteen years later a memo from the Division Engineer, Division of Safety of Dams to R.G. Henderson, general manager of the Malibu Water

Company, dated May 2, 1967 stated that an inspection of Malibu Dam in March of that year found the dam no longer impounded 15 acre feet of water, and according to the Water Code was no longer a dam within his jurisdiction. No further action concerning the dam would be taken by the division, nor would be required of Malibu Water Company.

The combination of disuse and a succession of floods and fires over the ensuing years have left the big steel irrigation pipes leading from the dam "high and dry" above the creek bed in many places. In others, large sections of the pipeline lie twisted and broken among the boulders that have washed down the creek. The watchman's little house at the east end of the dam was consumed by one of the devastating fires that raged through Malibu Canyon.

The Malibu Dam now is included in Malibu Creek State Park and the small amount of water in it is principally tertiary treated effluent from the Tapia Park sewage treatment plant. As for the dam - there it stands in front of practically 100 feet of solidly packed sand, silt and boulders, the accumulation of over 75 years' running of Malibu Creek.

Chapter 12

AGRICULTURE

Knowing of my interest in Malibu's history, my husband's friend, Horace J. Smith gave me a copy of his master's thesis "The Malibu Ranch."

He noted that in 1870 the United States Deputy Surveyor, in his report to Matthew Keller (then owner of Rancho Malibu) wrote, "The land's mild climate makes it particularly well adapted to the cultivation of all the tropical fruits – admirably adapted to the growth of coffee, tea, sugar cane, and cotton, as well as to corn, wheat, barley, and so forth. The tomato vine and all such tender plants flourish the whole year, blooming and bearing fruit to perfection, as well in the winter as in the summer."

The next date is 1898. The narrator now is Frederick Hastings Rindge, the next owner of Rancho Malibu. By this time the rancho had been made into a complete working ranch. In his "Happy Days in Southern California" Rindge describes how the ground is ploughed with the horses "Tom" and "Prince" and how the barley seeds are planted. He mentions his pride as owner sitting down to supper, the entire menu having been produced on the rancho. He writes of picking tangerine oranges, apricots, figs, and grapes. Animals at the rancho headquarters in Serra Canyon included: "Don Quixote" the donkey, sheep, 300 Angora goats, black pigs, chickens, peacocks and ducks as well as numerous hives of bees.

The cattle were out on the range except for the family's milk cows. Wild walnuts grew in Serra Canyon (as they do today wherever newcomers to California have not destroyed them). Rindge planted eucalyptus trees, (he knew Bishop William Taylor, who brought the first seeds from Australia) and mentioned they must be watered for two years and then will grow by themselves. The grevillias, palms, and most of the eucalyptus in Serra Canyon are "originals" from the Rindge days of the rancho.

Now let's skip to the 1920s. At that time there were nine Japanese farmers leasing land from Mrs. Rindge in the Malibu Creek delta. Kitaro Takahashi and his family came to Malibu in 1924 to grow vegetables on Mrs. Rindge's land. When the leases of the others expired, Mrs. Rindge did not renew them, leaving only Takahashi. At one time the family cultivated land on both sides of Malibu Creek and what is now known as Serra Road.

Amy Takahashi Ioki, youngest member of the family, was born in Malibu when the family lived in a house in Winter Canyon. When Pacific Coast Highway was rerouted up and over the hill and Winter Canyon was cut off, the Takahashi family moved to Westwood.

"Flowers, strawberries, cucumbers, tomatoes, string beans and celery – name it - and at one time or another we grew it," she told me. "Malibu Creek's delta has always produced good crops, except for the usual hazards."

Amy remembered so well one year when her father had acres and acres of peas, "beautiful green vines, carefully strung up and in full bloom. One of the fierce winds came up over night and flattened the whole crop."

Along with all other Japanese families in California, the Takahashis spent 1941 – 1945 in a concentration camp. But on their return, the eldest son, Kichi, and his younger brother, Maas, took over most of the responsibility for the farming, buying land on the west side of the creek when it went on the market.

The Takahashi brilliant red geranium garden attracted travelers along Pacific Coast Highway. Many even stopped to photograph the expanse of flowers. In fact on ski trips abroad I carried post cards of the geraniums to show fellow travelers the beauty of Malibu

Whether the crop was tomatoes, strawberries, or flowers, everyone in the Takahashi family worked – Uri, the twins Mary and Dorothy, and Amy as well as Kichi, Maas and the senior Takahashis. "We used to have some wonderful times in those early days," Amy remembered. At the time of my interview she was the wife of Min Ioki and mother of four grown children, three of whom had graduated from UCLA where daughter Nancy was a freshman that year.

Around the year 1939 another agriculturist on a large scale was working in Malibu – Al Thorne. Al had come from the farming area in the Deep South and found Malibu land superior for growing sweet corn. He leased large acreages of land all over Malibu - from Parker Mesa to Mulholland and grew corn. The family had a roadside stand on Jefferson Boulevard in Culver City where they sold the corn. In Malibu no barbecue or family reunion was complete without a boiler full of "Thorne's sweet corn."

Now in 2004 the Takahashi farmland rests beneath the Malibu Civic Center the Courthouse, the library and several government offices, with the weed-covered acreage at present known as the "Chili Cook-off" slated for development. But a few people still do remember those brilliant geranium fields.

Chapter 13

GOLD AND OIL

Freeman Kincaid, principal of Hollywood High School in 1900, hiked through the Santa Monica Mountains and found public land in the Trancas Canyon area bordering the Rancho Malibu. He and his four brothers and two sisters filed homestead claims and eventually owned 2,300 acres.

After reading favorable geological reports and learning of oil drilling in the Malibu ranch and in Carbon Canyon north of the rancho property, Mr. Kincaid decided in 1919 to drill on his property. The Liberty Oil Company (Freeman Kincaid and C.M. Decker among the members) put up its first rig on Kincaid's property at the top of Encinal Canyon. The wind promptly blew it down. The company replaced it with a steel-braced rig. All materials had to be hauled up the mountain roads by horse-drawn wagon, as there was no highway through Rancho Malibu.

My friend, the late Evelyn Kincaid Lippincott, told me her father pumped 10 barrels of oil a day. She didn't know how long the well was in operation, but says that when the Liberty Oil Company ran out of money, it quit.

The other oil ventures in Malibu were unsuccessful. In Carbon Canyon the well went down 55 feet, but was abandoned when it struck a "strong flow of gas." At "Point Duma" the well was drilled about a half mile from the ocean to a depth of 200 feet, when it struck water. The water rose 50 feet and the well was moved to another location on the mesa.

But one thing led to another and gold was discovered and mined on the Kincaid property.

I found out about this one day when I met Joe Kincaid in the market. He showed me the old newspaper he had been carrying in his back pocket.

Four-inch letters in black type proclaimed "GOLD FIND NEAR L.A.," backing even the sensational Arbuckle trial into second place on the *Los Angeles Record's* front page Friday, September 23, 1921.

I sat down and read: The discovery came by accident when oil prospectors sent their shale samples to Denver for assay. Reports came back with the startling news these samples assayed $14.50 to $40 a ton in flour gold. A succession of 50 assays revealed gold as high as $59.50 a ton and the story "leaked out" a week after the prospectors signed the lease.

The article described the Kincaid land and listed Nick Everett, "an old mining man" and Dr. W.T. Covington, a Los Angeles dentist, as partners in the venture. According to the newspaper, everyone was looking forward to a rosy future, with predictions running into millions of dollars for the gold and even, possibly, another gold rush.

No trace of gold had ever before been found in the Santa Monica Mountains. This discovery came about only when the ore was subjected to 480-degree heat, which was a tedious process and required a special laboratory. The partners estimated it would take only two dollars a ton to extract the gold.

But it wasn't that easy.

This was worth a real story now!

I called the *Santa Monica Evening Outlook* and next day their photographer met me, Joe and Evelyn at the Lippincott home above Trancas. Joe was just a little kid when the mining was going on, but he remembered how hard the men worked, digging the ore out of the tunnel. They had to load it on wooden-runnered sleds pulled by horses or donkeys. The old Model T trucks couldn't make it up the hill to the mine. Another crew unloaded the ore from the sleds to the trucks, which took it down to the ranch for another unloading - this time into the ball mill.

Joe was fascinated with the ball mill as a little kid. He described it as "a big cylinder with a whole lot of steel balls to roll around inside". The workers shoveled the ore into the cylinder and the big machine turned the cylinder as the steel balls rolled around, crushing the rocks until they were ground to dust as fine as flour. The flour came out of the cylinder through holes in the side – like a strainer or sieve. More workers shoveled the flour into sacks to take to the laboratory. Joe thought this was in San Bernardino. A chemist at Smith-Emery, one of the assay firms that did a report on the ore from Malibu, told me "so many dollars a ton" needs to be translated into the value of gold per ounce to determine the real worth of a strike. He added "In September 1921, the gold market fluctuated from a low of $26.88 to a high of $27.13 per fine ounce. Using the highest assay figure of $59.50 per ton against the value of gold at that time would indicate there was about two ounces of gold per ton of ore from the Malibu mine."

"But it turned out that the ore was not consistent," Joe said. "I remember my Dad talking about that with my uncles. At the laboratory they did what they called 'quartering.' They'd take 100 pounds of the ore and assay it in 25-pound lots. One would come out $25. Another would be 50 cents, another zero, and maybe the last would be 10 cents. That's what killed the deal in the end."

So the high hopes dwindled. The $25,000 facility to extract the gold from the ore on the spot never was built. The partners "just ran out of money and dropped the whole thing," Joe said, looking wistfully at the old newspaper spread out on the table.

Evelyn laughed as she held the last of the steel balls in her hand. "I rescued this from the fishpond where one of the grandchildren put it. It's awfully corroded and rusty now, but when I was a little girl I thought it was great sport to roll these balls downhill to the canyon. They were really shiny then."

What about the mine today?

Patting her half-coyote German shepherd dog, "Chew-shoe," Evelyn said. "There was a Malibu fire in 1935. It burned our house to the ground, and our father never did get over it. The sheriff made him leave, but he always thought he could have saved the place. In fires of other years he had saved a lot of other peoples' places and was known all up and down the mountains as a fearless firefighter. He died two years after the fire that took our house." Evelyn turned over a copy of a newspaper report of that devastating fire which she had saved in a scrapbook.

"Well, you know how it always rains so hard right after a big fire," Joe continued. The flood of 1935 washed down the mountain and took all of the tailings right down the canyon and out into the ocean.

"After the miners' money ran out and they left, we kids used to go into the tunnel once in a while. There was a little stream of water running down the floor of the tunnel and our ranch cattle used to come in there for water in the summertime."

"I remember the last time I was in that tunnel," Evelyn added. "Brrr... it was scary when a flock of bats flew over our heads."

At the time of this story, a shale slide completely covered the tunnel entrance, possibly the result of the flooding rains that followed the 1956 Malibu fire. Heavy chaparral liberally intertwined with poison oak made it a forbidding place.

"We were up at the mine a few weeks ago, a neighbor and I and two of his helpers. We brushed out a sort of trail. It's nothing but poison oak now. One of the helpers landed in the hospital, he got poison oak so bad, poor guy," Joe said ruefully.

"Now a young scientist thinks there might be a better way to get gold out of the rocks," Joe went on. "All he needs is a couple hundred pounds of the ore to experiment on. It might take three hours or it might take three days of hard shoveling to open up the tunnel again. It depends on how the stuff slides and how far back it's buried."

Neither Joe nor his sister were getting high hopes of becoming millionaires from that mine. On January 30, 1976 gold was $128.50 per fine ounce on the London market. The old assay would translate to $257.00 a ton.

But today's wages are even more inflated than the price of gold, so "El Dorado" in Malibu remains the dream it was so many years ago.

EPILOGUE

The *Santa Monica Evening Outlook* photographer who went with Joe, Evelyn and me climbed up through the chaparral to find the entrance to the mine. He landed in the hospital with a severe case of poison oak. Vandals have carried off all traces of the old oil well. Both Joe and Evelyn are dead and the Kincaid holdings have passed into other hands. The *Santa Monica Evening Outlook* has folded.

Chapter 14

THE FIRST NEWSPAPER - MALIBU BUGLE

1942

Unfinished, but "imposing," the "castle of Rancho Topanga Malibu Sequit" had just been purchased for use as a monastery by the Franciscan Order. The Las Flores Inn (present Duke's) still belonged to Messrs. Grimshaw and Golding. Malibu Mountain Inn (at the top of Latigo Canyon) advertised free archery lessons noting that "lunch may be procured." Art Jones' Malibu Inn Café and Cocktail Bar was "Open All Night." The Malibu Beauty Salon mentioned "reasonable rates" and "soft water." And Farley's Super Service at Malibu La Costa wrote "If you want your car to serve you for the duration, let us serve your car regularly."

These are some of the newsy notes in the columns and the advertisements in Malibu's very first newspaper – MALIBU BUGLE - from the May 15, 1942 issue, which is Volume I, Number 2.

I came across this fascinating publication one day when I was browsing through the Las Virgenes Library. The little four-page newspaper was a photocopy of a photocopy but I was fascinated to learn so much about what was going on in Malibu at the beginning of the "war years."

A surprising amount of information is packed into these four small printed pages. And in 1942 when people were forced to think not twice but three or four times before they traveled around on those precious rubber tires, the sheet must have been carefully read from front to back and saved as a precious reference.

In a box in the lower right hand corner of the front page, *Malibu Bugle* is listed as "Circulating in Topanga, Calabasas, Agoura, Cornell, Chatsworth, Lake Park, Decker, Latigo, Trancas, Encinal, Las Flores, Las Tunas, Malibu La Costa, and Malibu." Charles Lapworth of 23956 Roosevelt Highway, Malibu, or Box 94, Agoura, was editor and publisher. Subscription rates were "Twelve Months. $2.50. Single Copies, ten cents".. Acme Press of Santa Monica did the printing.

The *Malibu Bugle's* purpose was to disseminate news to the Civil Defense volunteers in the 300-square-mile Malibu Division, which stretched from Calabasas, Chatsworth and Topanga to every canyon and beach in Malibu. I cannot comprehend the organizational problems of finding Civil Defense volunteers in this vast area with its scattered population. Consider that many people went into war industry, went into the war itself, or couldn't use their cars because of the extreme shortage of rubber tires.

It was just five months since the beginning of World War II and it amazes me even more to read how Malibu already was organized. In addition to his Hollywood commitments, Warner Baxter headed the Ration Board and at the date of that publication had just straightened out federal regulations about tires, only to be confronted with the new rules about sugar. (My note: Wait until later when the meat and shoe regulations came out.)

Captain Jay Morley was debating about how to use the "Bearcat" siren just installed on the roof of the Malibu Court House. A Malibu Committee gave the needed "push" to get supplies for the casualty station in Topanga. There were five mounted patrols in the Malibu area, saving precious tires. A junior mounted patrol even took care of Topanga. Judge O. Benton Worley (later to be Malibu's Judge) chairman of the Calabasas sector, described it as "short on population, but long on patriotism."

I remember wondering about a large wooden "V" on the hillside in Agoura the first time we drove along Ventura Boulevard (before the freeway). The *Malibu Bugle* noted: "Chief Rolling Cloud, President of the American Indian Association, was principal speaker at the dedication of a large wooden "V" erected on the hillside south of Ventura Boulevard." (Mystery solved.)

Present day "Malibu Colony" was known as "Malibu Beach" and boasted the first Malibu Homeowners' Association with Mr. Jo Swerling the president. In 1942 he wrote in the *Malibu Bugle* that "All residents are to be invited to Mr. Fred Beetson's barbecue grounds for a feast" on July 4. He added that Mr. Morris Rosenberg would direct "other exhilarating enjoyments" and that a bulldozer and tractor would "roll into action shifting the drifted sand from the bulkheads."

I wasn't surprised to see the names of my friends Florence Harrison, Betty Smith, Nellie Webster, and Jeannette Gunn among the volunteers in the Malibu Casualty station in the Malibu Courthouse. From my own experience of organizing a "Victory Work Center" in Seattle, I could just picture the "Malibu gals" winding bandages, knitting "watch caps" and writing letters to servicemen as they chatted to each other, exchanging recipes and dreading the drive to Santa Monica in the blackout. The war years were still quite fresh in their minds when I met them in 1949, and we compared notes on "what did you do during the war?"

I have never been able to find another issue of the *Malibu Bugle*, but would like to see the firsthand report of the submarine sighted off Malibu Beach. Also, I wonder if there were any advertisements of "Home for Sale" as many people did sell their Malibu Beach homes for practically nothing as they fled the beach.

Chapter 15

MALIBU PLAY DAYS

Once upon a time, when Malibu was a "village" and everyone knew everyone else, the Malibu Township Council appointed me chairman of a summer festival "to include everybody." That was quite an order, but I got a group of friends together and we came up with "Malibu Play Days," chose a theme, and scheduled the first one for the first Saturday after the first full moon of August in 195...

We invited Malibu's businessmen, horsemen, firemen, and artists, Our Lady of Malibu Catholic Church, the Malibu Community Presbyterian Church, the Kiwanis Club, the Lions Club, the Optimist Club and all 25 homeowners' associations to spread the word around. They did.

The Saturday morning pet show brought out children and pets ranging from dogs, cats and birds to a donkey. Everyone was a winner. Malibu Lions Club men cooked hot dogs for all of the kids and Malibu firemen took them for a ride on a firetruck, complete with sounding the siren. In the meantime, over at the old Malibu Inn on Old Malibu Road other volunteers cleaned up the abandoned parking lot and set up tables and chairs in preparation for the potluck supper and square dance. In their homes Malibu's cooks made their best recipes of casseroles, salads, and desserts for the feast that night. Inside the Inn building, Malibu artists hung their paintings, set up their sculptures or floral arrangements, all ready for the grand opening. Late in the afternoon Al Thorne drove up with his pickup truck loaded with freshly picked sweet corn. Reeves Templeman and his crew of helpers shucked the corn while Max Couchois and his helpers fired up the army field kitchen to be ready to cook it. A group of girls came with baskets full of bright geranium blooms from the Takahashi Gardens and decorated the tables.

Families trooped in, most of them costumed according to the day's theme --"Wild West," "Indian Tribes," "South Seas," etc. Men put down the picnic hampers and went off to join their comrades while the women set out the feast: mouth-watering brown-topped meaty casseroles, crisp salads, fancy breads, and shimmering gelatins filled with pale pink shrimp or luscious fruit. By then the corn was cooked and slathered with Adohr Farms butter. Crowning the feast the dessert table boasted "mile high" angel food cakes, decadent chocolate cakes, "healthy" carrot cakes, tangy lemon bars, nut-filled brownies, and piles of chocolate chip cookies, topped off with steaming coffee or cold soda pop.

Is it any wonder the first two or three sets of the square dance lagged just a bit? But soon the tempo revved up and the dancing continued by the light of the full moon.

After church hours on Sunday morning the volunteer crew hosed down Crummer Field in preparation for the horse show and gymkhana. Horses arrived, some in trailers, some ridden across the fields from Serra Canyon stables, others ridden along beside the highway. (Once upon a time traffic was easy.) The Optimist Club readied the cantina (homemade hamburgers 25 cents), the electrician set up the announcer's system. Riders gathered at the top of the hill (present site of the Maison de Ville condominiums) for the Grand Entry behind a lead rider, maybe either Lawrence Welk or Malibu's honorary mayor Brian Donlevy carrying the American flag. The parade down the hill, the quick trot around the arena, the presentation of the colors---the show was on!

And what a show! The audience – many clinging to the fence around the arena – others sitting on the ground on a little hill -- shouted in encouragement to the fastest favorite. Events featured every kind of rider, from tots being led around the ring to riders on elegant five-gaited show horses, thrilling gymkhana races, and fine Thoroughbred jumping in what was then termed "English" classes.

But the day's festivities didn't end with the horse show. The sunset boat ride up and down Malibu's coast came next. We boarded the "Lenbrook" at the end of Malibu pier and saw our beach houses from a different view. Just as the summer sun seemed to go "kerplunk" into the ocean the boat docked and we went home, exhausted, once upon a time in Malibu.

Chapter 16

HAPPY DAYS IN CALIFORNIA

Rearranging one of my bookshelves the other day I came across Frederick Hastings Rindge's *Happy Days in Southern California* and couldn't resist taking time out to reread this memoir of Malibu more than 100 years ago. It's a paean of joy written by a humble and happy man. I found myself comparing the Malibu he knew with the one I enjoy.

Mr. Rindge's descriptions of beach life delighted me. Over a century ago he saw the same kinds of shells washed up on the beaches after storms; the sea birds that scuttled back and forth over the wet sand, picking out sand crabs as they followed the receding wavelets; the brown pelicans that sailed in majestic single file barely above the crests of breaking waves.

The man reveled in every aspect of his wide rancho, whether it was on the beach or in the canyons. He tells of the sycamores and oaks (the ones I see today probably are the same ones he saw) and describes how the chaparral grows again after a fire. His list of Malibu wildflowers is the same as mine: blue lupine, filaree, baby blue eyes, cream cups, and golden poppies for a start. And I am sure today's mustard grows so tall it would hide a man on horseback as it did the vaqueros on Malibu Rancho 100 years ago.

Mr. Rindge's joy in his home and family shines through as he writes graphic descriptions of the birds around the house. I share his pleasure in the linnets nesting in nooks and crannies around my garden as he did in his 100 years ago, and am equally fascinated by the antics of hawks descended from those he saw displaying aerial acrobatics over his fields.

His family was dear and interesting to him as he writes about the children rescuing an injured bird and their playing with their donkey, "Don Quixote." When he lists a dinner menu of food all produced on the ranch, you get a feeling of his pride and innate pleasure in the place.

Frederick Hastings Rindge was a religious and charitable man. His prose is not lyrical, but steady and descriptive, filled with Biblical references appropriate to the time in which he lived. His reverence for, and joy of life comes through in every chapter. His business acumen has been well documented, and were he alive today he would doubtless be called a "Renaissance Man." In the foreword to the reprinted edition of the original 1889 book his grandson, Ronald Rindge, describes his life. But this book is where he reveals much of his heart and soul where it lives -- in Malibu. I would like very much to have known him.

Chapter 17

Herve Babineau

Herve Babineau went to work for Art Jones in 1929. Malibu businesses then included Jones' real estate office and his Malibu Inn restaurant across the road from the "Malibu Movie Colony" Beach. The highway through Rancho Malibu had been open about three years. None of the Colony's many vacant lots were for sale and could be leased only through Jones.

In this 1988 interview, Herve told me that he did everything in the Malibu Inn from waiting on tables to managing the place. When 10 of the Colony houses were damaged in the 1929 fire, Herve helped to repair them. He said that as one of the boys in a large family in New Bedford, Massachusetts, his father had taught him how to do everything from plumbing to carpentry.

While working on the Colony houses Herve became acquainted with the owners, who soon hired him to do their routine repairs – from plumbing to fencing. He lived in a small apartment off the Colony beach, and "house-sat" various Colony beach houses during the winter months.

In the rainstorms of 1935-36 every Colony house from numbers 1 to 26 was under ocean water in the front and rainwater in the back. Herve described a literal lake in the low spot behind the houses. Backyards flooded when debris blocked the drain beneath the road.

Jones offered $25 per house to anyone who could get the water out. Herve devised a pumping system and simply pumped the water to the other side of the road. He said, "Jones paid up."

That 1935 repair job after the storm included putting a bulkhead in front of the houses. The first one required a 2x120-inch board fence dug into the sand two feet. Each year the water rolled over this wall and dug further into the sand. Each year the fence had to be made deeper – until it was down to 16 feet. Herve remembered that all that digging had to be done by hand.

On this project Herve got to know Louis Kunz, an engineer and carpenter from the motion picture studio, making repairs to Fred Beetson's beach house. (Beetson, Herve said, was the "official film censor," forerunner of the Hayes office). Shortly after, Kunz joined Babineau in his shop behind the Malibu Inn – in one of the houses that had been moved off the beach.

Kunz and Babineau became official partners when Herve went into the army during World War II. When he returned from Tokyo, they bought the old car barn, which had been the Rindge railroad terminal (across the highway from Malibu Pier but since demolished). They remodeled it, adding a two-story mid-section with two apartments – one for the Kunz family and one for the Babineaus.

The business was known as "Malibu Builders Supply" and carried everything for a prospective house builder: lumber, hardware, paint, electrical, and plumbing. By then Malibu real estate was "going to town." Houses sprang up like mushrooms all along the beach and clear out on Point Dume. Kunz sold his interest in 1957. The new owner sold the lumber department and leased space to a cabinet maker. Herve then sold his interest and went into the building business on his own.

By the time of my interview in his 60 years in Malibu, Herve Babineau had remodeled practically every house in Malibu Colony and several of them more than once or twice. He remembered among his clients: Adela Rogers St. John, Warner Baxter, John Gilbert, Connie and Joan Bennett, Lupe Velez, and Brian Donlevy, to mention a few. He specialized in meticulous woodwork with particular attention to the nice details.

In 1988 Herve still kept the Colony going. He knew the location of every shut-off valve, switch panel, septic tank and drain field. He did the first landscaping along the Colony roadside and on the day of this interview supervised the setting of another batch of trees along the entrance road.

Herve and his wife, Tobey, lived in the "only house in the Colony zoned for horses." But instead of a corral they made a flourishing green lawn with a rose garden, hibiscus and exotic flowering plants. A clear blue swimming pool with an unobstructed view of Serra Retreat on one side, Malibu Lagoon on the other made a tropical setting for their neat home.

In 1988 Herve predicted "There will be a lot of building, but the little guy will be taxed out. Who can afford to build when it costs $25,000 for a permit and to check out the land (geological and soil tests), $18,000 to get water connected, $2,000 for a meter, or $10,000 to $20,000 if it's a new meter, plus $1.50 a square foot for schools. It's about a $135,000 layout before a building even gets started!" He would be shocked at current rates!

Today if you look closely you will find a tree at the entrance to the Malibu Beach Colony lovingly dedicated to Herve Babineau for his more than 70 years of service.

Chapter 18

THE SEASONS

How many times has a friend from the east coast complained "But there are no seasons in California?" Maybe. But having lived In Malibu for more than 50 years I have discovered not just four seasons, but four CLIMATES!

Malibu is a 27-mile oceanfront, backed by the Santa Monica Mountains. It has woodsy canyons cutting down to the sea, several wide mesas and 27 miles of mountainous areas — an amazingly diversified place. Newcomers may be drawn here by any one of these terrains, yet are constantly surprised when they begin to explore all of Malibu.

Beach

If the sun is not your undoing, the beach is the ideal place to begin your life in Malibu, as it was mine. It's best to start with an early morning breakfast on the deck of a beach house. Smell the salty tang of the ocean breeze and watch the seabirds scurry back and forth to find the best sand crabs before they are covered by the next wavelet. Watch as an itinerant seal swims just beyond the surf, or perhaps a line of pelicans gracefully skims the water. Then it's time to lie down on the warm sand for a snooze to the music of the weaves and the cries of the birds.

This inaction soon calls for a quick run across the sand, and a dive into the cool water! Catch a breath and swim out beyond the breakers. Arms, legs, and breath synchronize. You're in euphoria! Return on a wave to hit the sand — invigorated and wonderfully refreshed.

Make beach walking any time of the day or night a favorite pastime, and inevitably, as every beach walker does, become a "beachcomber." The "loot:" interesting little stones, bits and pieces of driftwood, the odd shell, "gems" of tide-smoothed colored glass, black or white pebbles to add to a collection — always something. Go watch the surfers at famous "Surf Rider Beach," or a catamaran race off Zuma Beach, or an intrepid water skier skimming along in the wake of a speeding boat. Something interesting is always about to happen.

Yes, there is fog at the beach, and the piano strings do rust. It's a "high maintenance" area and the houses must be painted frequently. There usually isn't much ground but ingenuous gardeners grow flowers, fruit trees, and vegetables in pots. My friend Joan raises zucchini, squash, carrots, and cucumbers, as well as everything in the herb catalog, in a series of pots on the second-floor balcony.

Canyon Life

Instead of the allure of surf and sand, my true gardener friends are happiest in one of Malibu's canyons. They like the thought that some of the venerable native oaks and sycamores may have sheltered a Chumash ranchería, a Spanish vaquero tending a herd of mares, or cattle on Rancho Topango Malibu Simi and Sequit.

Canyon dwellers find the soil rich, and the climate right for growing every kind of exotic tree, shrub and flower. They are the ones who enjoy the changing seasons of the Northeast. They don't mind raking up the dead sycamores leaves in the fall, and their springtime begins when the green leaflets come out. Canyon greenhouses attract landscape artists from all over Southern California. Malibu boasts several internationally renowned orchid farms as well as some spectacular rose gardens.

Seeing the occasional raccoon, opossum, red fox, or wildcat is an excitement, but the many deer living in the canyons are less than welcome to my friend, Pat, whose large rose garden provides them with extra-special treats. Coyotes, rabbits, pack rats, and gophers are everywhere except on the sandy beaches. Canyon gardeners have to battle "critters" and a host of crawling and flying pests eager to feast on homegrown produce.

Bird lovers come to Malibu's canyons: flyways for migrating flocks of birds in the fall or spring. Tall trees make a haven for mockingbirds, while little red breasted house finches like to nest in eaves, hanging baskets and other small sheltered places around the house. Their lilting song is a lovely reward. Just about all flower gardens attract hummingbirds by the score, and a strategically placed feeder or two is well worth the trouble of keeping them filled. The bright cerise, sparkling green and shining gold of these little birds in the sunshine always fascinates me and is a sure-fire conversation piece.

Horse owners gravitate to the Malibu canyons, where several stables of show horses have private riding rings. "Back yard" horses in the canyons may have access to excellent riding trails. Most of my canyon-dwelling friends raise pets, especially those whose homes are on at least one acre of ground.

Canyons are the perfect place for children. They can climb trees, build forts and tree houses, and go exploring. Some canyons also have beach privileges. But those that do not are never too far from the public beaches at Zuma or Leo Carrillo.

The Mesas

My husband and I had not lived in Malibu long before we learned second only to the beach front, Malibu is famous for its "view property" on one of the mesas: Point Dume, Malibu Park, Carbon Mesa, Big Rock Mesa or Las Flores. From friends' living rooms we could see "beyond forever." The vast blue of the ocean and islands stretching below often transfixes me. From another living room's panorama the whole Santa Monica Bay spreads out in the darkness, ringed with lights. From others Catalina Island looms as the center of attraction. Adding to the mesas' lure are the mountains rising in the background. With the changing light, their green or brownish vegetation may go from blue black to smoky lavender. Mesa sunsets' surreal colors may range from the palest lemon yellow to the darkest deep purples and reds, lighting up the whole sky.

"Windswept" describes Malibu's mesas, even today when trees planted in the late 1940's have matured and provide shelter from all but gale-force blasts. But aside from the wind, weather on the mesas is pleasantly mild without much of the beaches' dampness. To those who dwell here, the spectacular ocean views make up for any disadvantages.

Every place in Malibu is just minutes from a beach and mesa dwellers take advantage of this at all times of the year as do those of us who live still farther beyond in the mountains.

Top of the Malibu

From our mountain top we have wider and higher views and can see beyond miles and miles of blue water to the "Slipper Island" (Santa Barbara) and 74 miles farther out, San Nicolas Island, and the shipping lanes in between. Then we just turn around and look at the varied skyline of shaggy or jagged peaks, the pink rocks on Boney Ridge and the shading in the canyons in the ever-changing light.

When fog from the beach creeps up the canyons, it fills them with billowy white clouds, leaving just the tips of the higher mountains showing, like islands in a gigantic steaming volcanic lake. Sunsets from our mountain house are more than spectacular. We have the feeling of being "higher than the sun" as it slips down behind a hill and lights the sky with every shade of every color of the rainbow.

Like ours, houses in the mountains have to be carefully engineered and located away from the path of an old arroyo seco that suddenly springs to life in an especially hard winter rainstorm. Also the building must be on solid ground that will not slide after a heavy rain.

But the prime concern in the mountain area is to make a house as fireproof as the current technology permits – no exposed wood, or shake roof, water available immediately (as in the swimming pool where a little pump can be used to spray stray sparks), fire retardant plantings and the chaparral cleared at least as far away as the fire department requires.

Our mountaintop has the poorest soil possible for gardening. We brought topsoil from the bottom of a dry lake up along Yerba Buena and put down a sod lawn. In two weeks the rabbits had consumed all of the beautiful green grass. Next year we thought the rabbits were almost gone, but no. Another year we tried planting seeds, with the same result. We gave up and have spaces of lovely California earth between plantings of rabbit-proof shrubs. Citrus and avocados thrive on a sunny slope where there seldom is frost. Birds feast on the ripening almonds and plums. We built a bird-proof cage around a thriving fig tree, only to have it destroyed by gophers. But the olallie berries thrived under a bird proof cover.

Yucca plants which early Spanish explorers named "Candles of the Lord" and later cowboys called "Spanish bayonets " grow all over Malibu land. When the first one came up and bloomed in our patio I discovered both descriptions to be true. The white plumes of blooms atop a long stalk did resemble a huge candle, and the plant's sharp spines were lethal to me, the careless gardener. I also discovered that the flowers are fluorescent and gleam at night attracting fragile white moths which come for their nectar and pollinate them.

The bonus for leaving the beach for the mountains is the birds. There are myriads of them. Many mornings and evenings, one or two coveys of quail make their sedate way across the yard to the water dishes. Towhees flit among the bushes or enthusiastically splash in the birdbath. In summer golden orioles help themselves at the hummingbird feeders and brown thrashers and warblers sing their lilting songs from the tallest eucalyptus. Hundreds of meadowlarks winter in our plowed field. Western flycatchers ("top notch birds" at our house) greet the spring mornings with a pert "What Cheer." Crows cruise around, their bright eyes seeking anything edible on the ground, and the resident roadrunner spends hours fighting his reflection in a mirrored glass door. A graceful red-tailed hawk soars above the sycamore tree, casing out last year's nest. From March to September swallows dip water from the pool for their cliff dwellings.

We mountain dwellers hear coyotes yap at all hours of the day and night as they chase after rabbits. Occasionally we have seen a badger whiffle across the patio to dig out a literal shower of dirt at a gopher hole on the bank. Sometimes the wildcat comes to drink from the pool. Other times I see him hunting along the driveway. Deer come and go year-round and sample various "delicacies" in the garden. One afternoon a stately mountain lion inspected areas between chaparral and plowed ground while my neighbors and I watched transfixed. But we breathed sighs of relief when he nonchalantly sauntered back into the bushes.

Sometime between early January and late February the white ceanothus comes into full flower bringing the hillsides alive with gleaming bushes of snowy white blooms. If there has been plenty of rain, wild flowers appear like magic on one-day bare ground, a few days later red, yellow, pink, white, or blue blossoms along the roadside (if the county hadn't sprayed at the end of summer). Beside the walk along our driveway I have counted

26 different blooms from wild roses and bright Spanish pinks to tiny purple filaree and golden California poppies.

As everywhere in Malibu except on the beach, there are horse farms in the mountains where favorite trail rides are easily accesible. Riders trailer their mounts to Malibu Creek State Park for a grueling 25-mile trek up to the ridge above Pepperdine and back. Runners and cyclists share the roads in the early mornings and evenings. It's a hikers' paradise. Trails lead up and over to Boney Ridge or out to the edge at Charmlee Park. Runners also find some spectacular routes through Malibu Creek State Park.

Our climate here includes HOT days in summer, tempered by afternoon breezes from the ocean. Once every few years we get a bit of snow or enough frost to make the bare branches of trees look as if encased in glass or to put a sheet of ice on the Jacuzzi. When gale force winds spring up from the northeast, tree branches crash and things blow off roofs from shingles to copper trimmings. The fireplace smokes and the sliding doors rattle in their pockets. It's spooky, but doesn't last long.

Malibu is a universe of its own. And that's why we live here!

Chapter 19

HOLIDAYS

Our Christmases in Seattle and New England had always centered on a fragrant green fir tree. In 1949 we were really looking forward to our first Christmas in Malibu, even though the weather seemed to us more like April than December.

About three days before Christmas my husband brought home a little fir tree, just the right size for our small apartment. We stood it in front of the window that overlooked the deck, with a view of the ocean peeking through. I ransacked the cupboards to find any decorations left over from other years and had them ready for our Christmas Eve "decorating celebration."

After trying to see the ocean behind the tree we decided to move it to another corner of the living room. When my husband set it down in the new location all of the needles fell off, and there it stood, a silhouette of naked branches. That was the last cut tree we ever had in Malibu.

By the next Christmas we were living in a house and had collected driftwood along Carbon Beach. I had been using one piece with a nice sculptural shape as a living room decoration. Instead of using a traditional Christmas tree, I draped some bright beads and a few shiny colored balls on this piece, and that was our "tree."

Several of my beachcombing neighbors were artists and all of us looked for interesting things every time we walked the beach. In addition to pieces of driftwood we often found shells of every description. Once in a while there would be a large green glass globe, a real treasure from a deep sea fishing boat's net. We hoarded these goodies in boxes on our beach decks for use as table decorations all year.

One year Alice Rinaldi found the full size stem of a century plant, complete to the dried seedpods. The stiff bloom part was triangle shaped, perfect for a Christmas tree. Alice gilded the entire stalk, including the seedpods. These were flat, so she put the ornaments on them: gilded shells, mussels and a few little rock crab skeletons she had found on Carbon Beach. The whole thing looked rather stark, so she wrapped it loosely in gold net for an ethereal effect. She put her "Century tree" on display in the Presbyterian church bazaar. It sold for the wonderful sum (in the 1950's) of $25! So, next year all of us watched the gardens as we drove around Malibu, to spot any blooming century plants. We begged them for our project. Again we sold every "Century tree" we made.

Next year we concocted Malibu Beach wreaths. We bought plastic foam wreath bases of varied sizes. For true Malibu decorations we used the shells, sand dollars, and small crab shells we'd gathered. First we gilded the styrofoam wreath shape: either gold or silver. Then we attached the decorations. We wrapped the whole thing in gold or silver net, and there was the Malibu Christmas wreath! These too were "hot items" at both the Presbyterian and Our Lady of Malibu church bazaars.

One year we had an "angel factory" in our picnic place. To make an angel we used a cylinder and an egg shape ball of plastic foam plus a coat hanger, cardboard cut out wings, strands of yarn for hair and a square of an old bed sheet dipped in glue. When put together according to the directions and sprayed, either gold or silver, these materials made lovely angels. For many years the Malibu Presbyterian Church Christmas tree was decorated with glittering baubles, all hand made by the women of the Guild. Part of the fun of these was going around the tree to find "yours" from year to year.

Then came live trees. They were best of all, as after each Christmas we'd plant our tree (or trees) somewhere on our property. Today a gigantic pine shades a picnic place and many others grow along the driveway.

Malibu Thanksgiving dinners at our house often have been picnics under the oak tree or on the beach. It depended on the November weather. It was easy to pack the dinner in the back of my little Datsun station wagon and unload it under the oak tree down in the field below the house. It was near enough so the hot food was hot and the cold cold. A beach picnic just meant taking the food out of the house and setting up a buffet on the deck. Guests could walk down the steps balancing their plates and sit on driftwood facing the ocean. But we had to warn out-of-towners not to feed the seagulls until the picnic was over!

The "frosting on the cake" of every Malibu Thanksgiving or Christmas at the beach was a minus tide, i.e. lower than the mean average tide. Everyone took off shoes and socks and walked out toward the sunset. Seabirds scuttled before us, the small waves curled easily onto the wet sand. The runners took off and the others followed at a leisurely pace. Thanksgiving and Christmas dinners on the hill usually ended with a cup of coffee in hand, out by the pool watching the sun go down and the sky light up in rainbow colors. Either way it is MALIBU!

Chapter 20

CONTROVERSIES

Let one of Malibu's celebrities disagree with one or more of Los Angeles County or California Coastal Commission edicts and there are columns of newsprint in papers and magazines around the world. I even get clippings from friends as far away as Boston and Seattle. "Controversy, thy name is Malibu" could be our motto over the past two hundred years.

It must have been prophetic, as an argument brought about the first historical record of Malibu in 1805. (See my chapter on Tapia's 1805 petition). His offending neighbor, Suniga, is never heard of again, and Don Jose seems to have been at peace with numerous relatives who had settled on his rancho.

Successive owners found it necessary to evict "many Tapias," until by 1876, when Henry Keller owned the rancho, all had departed.

Keller permitted homesteaders on the public lands behind the rancho to pass across his property to their claims if they chose to approach them via the precarious route along the beach from Boca de Santa Monica.

Successive "land booms" brought more and more people to California, among them many hunters and fishermen seeking the bountiful deer, quail, and doves in the upper reaches of Rancho Malibu. Frederick Hastings Rindge, the newest owner, allowed them to cross his property for a while. But when the fishermen disturbed the watering holes of his cattle, and when some of the hunters slaughtered steers instead of deer, Rindge closed the rancho, giving gate keys to bona fide homesteaders only.

Several barred people objected to the locked gates and controversy flared, with homesteaders maintaining it was their "right" to pass freely through the rancho.

Litigation began in earnest soon after Rindge's untimely death at age 48 in 1905. The Southern Pacific Railroad was planning to run tracks through Rancho Malibu to connect with the Santa Monica spur. May K. Rindge, the widow, had completed a narrow gauge private railroad for transporting hides, grain, etc., through the 22 mile rancho. She finally won this lawsuit when the judge ruled the place "did not need two railroads."

Shortly before his death, Rindge had a crude wagon road built from Boca de Santa Monica to the eastern boundary of his rancho (at Las Flores). By 1915 Nellie and John L. Webster were among several families who had fishing camps in Las Flores Canyon. The Grimshaw & Golding store (on the site of the present Duke's restaurant) stocked a few groceries and provided home cooked meals for venturesome motorists who braved the two-lane road to the "turn around and go back" gates at the Las Flores entrance to the rancho.

These gates finally officially opened to through traffic in 1928, and Malibu started to become a "place" when other moving picture stars followed Anna Q. Nilsson's example and leased land on the beach in what soon became known as "Malibu Moving Picture Colony." Today's "Colony" is still a popular address for stars of the entertainment world.

Marblehead Land Company formed to handle land sales. Gradually portions of the rancho opened for development: Malibu La Costa Beach and hillside first, then Carbon Mesa and Carbon Beach, Broad Beach, and later Point Dume, Malibu Park, Sycamore Meadows, etc.

Wartime made a real hazard for Malibu residents. Rumors of Japanese submarines just off the coast caused many people to flee to inland locations. Anti-aircraft batteries in the mountains, a complete blackout and strict gasoline rationing were all parts of the war effort. Some of the residents who remained worked at the Douglas Aircraft plant in Santa Monica or volunteered for Red Cross activities in the Malibu sheriff's station. But the school buses ran regularly to Santa Monica and life went on.

My 1949 introduction to Malibu type controversy came when I read that some Malibu people objected to naming the new elementary school for Judge John L. Webster. In 1950 the post office arrived. Before that, all box holders had to trek to Pacific Palisades for their mail. Natural gas lines were installed in 1944. Soon more restaurants, a grocery store and real estate offices began to appear.

From the early 1940s homeowners associations sprang up like mushrooms: Big Rock Mesa, Malibu Beach, Trancas Beach, Malibu La Costa, and West Malibu Community Council, all very actively arguing over zoning and deed restriction violations. The Malibu Township Council formed in 1947 to create a more unified "Malibu front" for doing business with the Los Angeles County Board of Supervisors. Residents elected Ralph Lamb as the first chairman.

Malibu's water supply became a concern in 1946. Then most of the water came from wells in various canyons belonging to the Malibu Water Company. During one very dry summer, several of the Malibu wells pumped seawater. In 1954 residents finally realized the canyon wells were insufficient, and voted to join the Metropolitan Water District.

But the problem of actually bringing Metropolitan Water to the area created an acrimonious battle of words when Los Angeles County proposed a 30-inch pipeline from Charnock Wells in Culver City to the Ventura County line at a cost of $7,800,000 to be paid by a tax on land only.

The September 15, 1959 election passed the measure by 99 votes. Dire predictions that "large numbers of citizens" would "go broke under the tax burden" and that the tax itself was "utterly immoral" were unfounded. On October 23, 1959 Malibu and Topanga officially became Los Angeles County Waterworks District 29.

Dissatisfaction with the Los Angeles County Board of Supervisors came to a head in the early 1960s and the first try at incorporation began. Once again the community was polarized. This time the "Noes" won, as they did again in the 1970s. It took 20 more years for Malibu to finally become an official city. And with multiplicity of civic responsibility came a multiplicity of controversies. Here is one:

Sometime in the 1960s a group of farsighted citizens began a campaign to get a sewer system for Malibu. The water dispute of a few years before was like a "sparkler" compared to a "rocket bomb" when it came to the heated disputes this project generated. Sewers went down to defeat. And now, after over 40 years and at least two more "tries" the idea of sewers still has the community in an uproar. In the meantime, both costs and bacteria count are escalating.

But when the concept of a freeway through Malibu surfaced, the community united against the route through Malibu Canyon that would empty "all of San Fernando Valley" onto PCH. This project was abandoned. The state anticipated a freeway and had purchased several properties in various canyons before the project failed.

A proposed nuclear reactor to be located at the mouth of Corral Canyon similarly brought Malibu citizens together against it. The site was a confirmed geological hazard. The west wind would drift possible radioactivity from an accident out across the San Fernando Valley and insurance companies denied any kind of compensation. The reactor was abandoned as unfeasible.

As for "in Malibu" projects, the arguments go on. Somehow it's always "us" against "them" no matter what is proposed. Bones of contention have been the equestrian center in Malibu Park, another sewer plan, softball fields, a senior center, countless battles with the California Coastal Commission over public access through private property to the beach, building moratoriums, etc., as well as practically any proposal that might bring anyone else or another business to Malibu. Arguments wage in city council meetings and lawsuit after lawsuit is brought, often even by the council itself.

In some quarters of Malibu the televised city council meetings are an evening's entertainment. People in other areas of the country have their differences, but seem for the most part to conduct themselves a bit more courteously than Malibu people do. I can understand why the County Board of Supervisors always dreaded the "Malibu confrontations." These now take place at the meetings of our own city council.

Letters to the Editor in both the *Malibu Surfside News* and the *Malibu Times* are rife with what to me seem to be libelous accusations on practically every project the city council proposes. At election time the pages fairly sizzle. Property development seems to inspire the most ire, with Coastal Commission interference and taxes coming in close behind. Is this attitude because so many people have come to Malibu "to get away from it all" and suddenly discover "it" is here in Malibu too?

Chapter 21

MUSTARD

There is a legend that an early mission padre dropped mustard seeds along the way so explorers could find the way back to their convent in Mexico, and that is why wild mustard grows all over Southern California.

We came to Malibu after years in Washington and Massachusetts where (except for the Washington rhododendrons) wildflowers are not especially spectacular.

In the spring soon after we moved to Carbon Beach the empty land across the highway burst into bloom with a solid mass of bright yellow mustard. I always tried to have the house filled with flowers, but we didn't have a garden, just potted plants in the patio. So seeing the beautiful yellow mustard blooms on their "artistic" stems, I picked a large bouquet, put it in an elegant green glass vase and set it in the living room where I was doing my reading for classes at UCLA.

In the dim consciousness of my surroundings, I felt my nose closing. I could hardly breathe, but I smelled something unpleasant. The odor became so persistent I got up and "cased the joint." I found the culprit my beautiful bouquet of mustard. I took it out and dumped it into the ocean. And that's the last time I've picked mustard.

The following spring I found a more practical side of mustard in Malibu. One bright Saturday morning as I went out to water the hibiscus by the fence I noticed a group of people digging plants on the land across the highway. To satisfy my curiosity I went over to talk to them. They were digging wild mustard for the greens. "Haven't you heard of mustard greens?" one lady asked me. Yes, but I considered the greens in the market in about the same category as spinach and didn't pay any attention to them. "These are fresh and good," the lady assured me. Every spring before the Engles built their house on the property people came to dig the greens. We called them "the mustard people."

Mustard must be indestructible. Nobody wants it in the garden, and no matter how many times it's cut back, it always returns the next year. But when the spring rains are right, the hills around Corral Canyon burst into golden bloom with masses of mustard from the edge of the highway up to the summit, and I need sunglasses to look at the shining brilliant color. I remember the day I walked up that hill with my friend Natalie. She set up her easel, brought out her paints and went to work. I wandered around, sneezing, among the flowers, many taller than I, trying for the perfect angle for photographs.

Natalie's painting appeared in a Malibu artists exhibition. My photographs probably went in letters to Washington and Massachusetts. But the mustard blooms every spring and I always think of that lonely homesick padre scattering seeds.

Chapter 22

THEN CAME PEPPERDINE!

When we first came to Malibu there were more horses than people in most canyons, so as a matter of course, Ed and I became horse owners too. Our stable featured American Saddlebred show horses, but my own special horse was a little strawberry roan Morgan named "Sally." She was a trail horse, and my friend Sharon and I often rode from Serra Canyon up and over onto the surrounding mesas. One day we took a cattle trail through a tunnel under Malibu Canyon Road and up into the mountains. We stopped on a promontory overlooking the Malibu Lagoon. What a view! The creek meandering between lush green banks; the shimmering blue ocean; and flat-topped Point Dume spread out before us. We mused, "What will become of this place?"

Ten years later - Pepperdine!

My husband and I were overjoyed! Malibu would be a college town! Not long after groundbreaking ceremonies on April 13, 1971, red tile-roofed light beige buildings began to appear on the hillside.

Seaver College Dedication Day, April 20, 1975 earned a gold-star on our calendar. What a thrill to see a dream come to life!

Our introduction to Pepperdine activities was "Kismet" performed dinner-theater style in the school's cafeteria complete to a camel parade on the outdoor terrace. Later, with the opening of Smothers Theatre on the campus, live entertainment came to Malibu. We particularly enjoyed all of the professional-level student productions ranging from *Music Man*, with professors' children as extras, to *Man of La Mancha* featuring John Raitt as both leading man and director. Smothers Theatre manager, Marnie Mitze continues to bring programs of wide appeal. And we don't have to drive 50 miles to see them!

The Fred Weisman Museum, right here in Malibu, shows exhibits of such world-renowned artists as Wayne Thibaud and Jimmy Ernst, works from the extensive Weisman collections as well as the works of student artists and members of the Malibu Art Association.

As our interests mostly were music, Ed and I started a recital series to present student musicians to the public, and brought our International Classical Guitar Competition to Pepperdine as well. World-renowned classical guitarist, Christopher Parkening, is the newest addition to the music department, already celebrated for the opera workshop directed by former Metropolitan Opera tenor Henry Price.

Pepperdine won worldwide television coverage during the 1984 Olympic Games as host for the water polo contest. But we found it more exhilarating to join the peppy basketball and volleyball fans flocking to Firestone Fieldhouse to cheer the "Home Team." Unexpectedly one night on a TV program in Philadelphia, we watched Pepperdine's baseball team win the national title.

Pepperdine does not fund a collegiate track program, but did have a dirt track. Being runners, my husband and I often trained on that dirt track and found it sub-par, especially after a rain. Thinking of something we could do for the whole Malibu community, we funded a regulation eight lane surfaced track. We enjoyed running on that fabulous surface so much we encouraged other runners to join us. This has become an informal track club as well a group of very special friends.

I became involved in some of Pepperdine's cultural activities with Rosemary and John Raitt when they started the Center for the Arts Guild. We planned to bring schoolchildren to Pepperdine to introduce them to theater. The guild's fundraising projects give money for special morning performances by groups doing Smothers productions suitable for children. It warms my heart to see youngsters react to music and dance, often for the first time in their young lives. Sometimes it's even surprising, as one morning a little boy about 9 or 10 years old walked into the theater, saw the red-curtained stage, turned to me and asked, "Where is the screen?"

The Art Guild encourages schools to have the children visit the museum, where Curator Michael Zakian teaches them about the paintings. The ArtsReach program began with just one performance. Now (in 2004) we have two full-house performances (a total of 1,000 children) for each program, there often is a waiting list! I am constantly amused at the way the children react to a program swishing their hips, attempting an acrobat's movements, making clown faces, imitating drumbeats. It's never ever dull! The guild's latest project brings some of the performers into a school for a "hands-on" demonstration. The possibilities are endless.

In summertime the Pepperdine campus fairly hums. You may see hundreds of children acting like little jumping jacks at "Basketball Camp" on the parking lot beside Firestone Fieldhouse. On the track's infield there might be flocks of screaming little girls chasing innumerable soccer balls. That's "Soccer Camp." Or in late afternoon you could meet a string of bedraggled little people carrying tennis racquets on their way up the stairs to the dormitories after a session of "Tennis Camp." On other days The Raleigh Runnels pool is awash with beginning young swimmers. On weekends, Mom, Dad and the kids enjoy a lively family swim. During the entire year Pepperdine's athletic facilities, including the weight room, tennis courts, and swimming pool, announce special times for community use. And you don't have to drive to town.

While my program includes no athletic activities beyond the track, I am very much interested in the Payson Library, which also is open to the Malibu community. I have found information on several research projects, and not being a student, needed a lot of help finding my way around the stacks. The cheerful and courteous library staff brought out many items not even on my list. Most of these I would have had to wait several weeks to secure from the public library.

Little Staufer Chapel has an entire wall of exquisite stained glass that always inspires a special trip to show to our out-of-town visitors. On a sunny afternoon the place fairly glows. To me it's the most beautiful place in Malibu for a wedding. But our great-niece, Lisa, chose a giant coral tree in Alumni Park as the setting for her wedding to Adam Burt on a beautiful September afternoon.

I have mentioned the Pepperdine activities in which I am personally involved. Pepperdine is much more than that. Compared to the state Universities, Pepperdine is small, but consistently ranks at the top of academic surveys. Its faculty includes distinguished nationally and internationally known professors in diverse fields from law to music. Students come from all over the world and Pepperdine young people have the opportunity to study in several world campuses, from Heidelburg, Germany and London, England to Sao Paulo, Brazil and Florence, Italy.

Pepperdine brings so many plusses to Malibu, but there is one more: I know the new Drescher Campus graduate school on the hill also has added housing for more students and faculty, but to me the jewel of the entire Pepperdine complex is the Hero's Garden, unobtrusively fronting a set of elegant buildings. It is in memory of Pepperdine alumnus, Thomas

Burnett, who perished in the 9/11 debacles, a quiet place for meditation. Birds flit among the new leaves of a young sycamore tree. A soft breeze stirs the Flag. I sit by the still pool facing the ocean, and look to infinity.

Pepperdine University...
"Smog-free, sun-kissed,
ocean-washed, island-girded,
and mountain-guarded."

M. Norvel Young

Chapter 23

EARLY CHURCHES

The war was over and by 1946 in Malibu, as everywhere in the country, life had returned to "normal." The Marblehead Land Company's enticing brochures brought families to live here. Malibu changed from summer beach vacation spot to a year-round community. True to American tradition, families needed churches.

One Sunday in 1946, a group of devout Catholics invited the Rev. Dan Gallagher, pastor of St. Jarlath's parish in Topanga, to come and say 8 a.m. mass for them in the Malibu Courthouse. Immediately after mass Father Gallagher had to jump into his old black Chevy and head up the road for the 9 a.m. mass at St. Jarlath's. Thus began the parish of Our Lady of Malibu Catholic church.

Three years later, dedication services opened Our Lady of Malibu church at the present site on Winter Canyon just off Malibu Canyon Road. When Father Gallagher was reassigned, Rev. Joseph Burbage came to Malibu. Under his guidance Our Lady of Malibu School began in 1958. On his untimely death in 1959 the parish direction passed to Monsignor Dennis Flavey.

The devastating 1970 fire destroyed Our Lady of Malibu convent and half of the sanctuary building. Monsignor John Sheridan led the flock through rebuilding that enlarged the sanctuary as planned before the fire. Our Lady of Malibu continues to grow and be a vital part of the Malibu community.

On Sundays for a few months in 1949 Our Lady of Malibu shared the Malibu Courthouse with the little congregation of the Malibu Community Presbyterian Church. The 8 a.m. Catholic mass preceded the 9 a.m. Presbyterian Sunday school. My husband and I joined this congregation sometime during the three years the church met there.

Down through the years I have attended some impressive church services all over the world, but the one that stands out in my memory is that 1951 Christmas Eve in the new Malibu Presbyterian Church. The sanctuary was bare except for the Celtic cross carved by Pastor Rodney McQuary and the sturdy altar built by Oscar Carlson. Children sat on their parents' laps to give seats to the grown-ups. The room was packed to the walls. That first simple candlelight service became a Christmas Eve tradition along with the singing of "The Halleluiah Chorus" from Handel's *Messiah*.

These two churches became the center of Malibu women's activities, with rummage sales, bazaars, lunches, fashion shows, teas, suppers, recitals and lectures. Religion didn't matter. Everyone supported all of the events. For Malibu's year-round residents these were "Society." (Note: observation of a reconsituted society editor)

New people brought different spiritual needs. In 1956 the first congregation of St. Aidan's Episcopal Church met in a stable on Point Dume. It survived moves to Trancas Restaurant, to Hughes Research Laboratories, and to the Schirmer Orchid Garden's lath house before the church opened on Pacific Coast Highway opposite Paradise Cove. David McKee and Son were contractors for the building, dedicated in April of

1961. The Rev. Jack Carlson began as first minister, followed by Father Lougee, under whose guidance St. Aidan's nursery school opened in 1962. Parishioners burned the mortgage in 1976 with the church's consecration and the opening of the new Joe Schiro Parish hall. The parish continues to grow under the direction of Rector Susan Klein.

On January 7, 1962 Juan Cabrillo School became the setting for another congregation – the Malibu United Methodist Church. Esther and Harry Lawry hosted the congregation in their home when the school rebuilt the auditorium. The Methodists went back to the refurbished auditorium until the new church dedication.

The A.I.A. award-winning chapel, designed by Richard Dorman, has a brilliant stained glass window by Malibu artist and ceramist Toby Schreiber. The elegant chapel was consecrated March 27, 1966. More buildings accommodated the growing congregation, among them a nursery school and social hall open for a host of youth activities and community affairs, The annual "Cook's Tour" brings out Malibu's "foodies" to sample the varied cuisines as well as those of us who enjoy seeing the architectural artistry of the homes on the tour.

Malibu First Church of Christ Scientist held services in the Malibu Courthouse from 1952 until the dedication on March 14, 1976 of the modern building on Pacific Coast Highway near Kanan-Dume Road. With the opening of Pepperdine University another religious group came to Malibu, the Churches of Christ. The congregation continues to hold regular services in Elkins Auditorium on the campus, as it has outgrown the Stauffer chapel. The chapel with its marvelous stained glass "Tree of Life" wall and six side windows forms a favored setting for weddings and a "must see" site for visitors to the Malibu campus.

As Malibu grows, religious needs multiply and now include Chabad of Malibu, Jehovah's Witnesses, Malibu Jewish Center and Synagogue, and the Vineyard Christian Fellowship.

Chapter 24

JIMMY DECKER

2003:

"A rock the size of a Volkswagen rolled down the mountainside and landed on the highway, just missing the morning traffic through Malibu Canyon," came a dispatch on the morning news.

This reminded me of another "rock episode" on Pacific Coast Highway years ago. A gigantic rock hung perilously over the highway, threatening beach houses below. The property owner was in New York when he got notice of the rock. He called Malibu's "Dynamiter" Jimmy Decker to take care of it. The project "hit the news" and people in Malibu had their say. Some that it was not endangering anything, others that it should be removed before there was a serious accident. Jimmy "took care of it" and years later he told me just how.

"That slab of rock was 16 by 14½ feet and was 9½ inches thick. It weighed 130 tons and was lying 185 feet straight up from Pacific Coast Highway, 210 feet from the highway, measured on the ground. I planned to dissolve the rock on the hill but needed dirt down along the highway and a high board fence to protect the houses when some of the pieces slid down. The state turned me down. Then the TV cameras got into the act. The state awarded the contract to Atkinson and Pollock, and in the end they did it my way. I wound up as the 'consultant' and finally broke up the rock.

"It took just one pound of dynamite. We drilled four holes in a square with a fifth in the center of the square. We used 14½ ounces to break the rock into four pieces: two ounces in the bottom of the holes at six feet, and one ounce in the holes at three feet with four ounces in the center hole.

"The rock dissolved and only a few pieces skittered down the hill, coming to rest behind the board fence. (Note: the fence still stands on Pacific Coast Highway).

"There was so much publicity, yak-yak and furor, I know a lot of people still think the rock wasn't any danger. I have pictures to show that it actually did move, and was ready to fall anytime. There was only one small rock holding it on the hill."

"Dynamiter"

The very word conjures up a secretive, shifty, furtive person, working stealthily undercover, completely opposite of Jimmy Decker, one of the 12 qualified explosive experts in Southern California. You would have to look far to find someone more straight-forward, communicative, and open-handed than Jimmy Decker, son of the late Atha Earl and Florence Decker (distant cousins of the original Decker settlers).

How did he become a dynamiter? He leaned back in his chair and his face took on a "remembering" look as he told me that as a boy he worked with Atha, his father, watching and helping dynamite rocks and hauling them away by horse team. The senior Mr. Decker, a distant relative of Marion Decker, built Mulholland Highway up from the beach to "past Mason's place" in the late 1920s. But Jimmy's first "solo" job was shooting the well for "Wasmer" near the present Camp for the Blind, then known as "Trail's End Ranch."

Hunting, fishing, working with his trees, including an avocado the size of Santa Barbara's famous Moreton Bay Fig, no alcohol and no tobacco, kept Jimmy a young 62 (in 1980 at the time of this interview). He had no patience with "those old men and women of 30 who come up to the country for a weekend and spend the time in the house watching some pro game on TV."

Jimmy's scariest job? "Cutting a road above the tunnel at the back side of Zuma Canyon. Below us was a sheer bluff and we had to shoot a "blow out."

"We could look up and see daylight through the hole, and then had to go up through it, hanging on by our fingernails with nothing but air below!" Jimmy looked a little grim, just remembering.

Another "bad one" at Black Point, Mugu, resulted in the death of one of the men. Jimmy transferred to Ojai.

One "ticklish" demolition job Jimmy did in Ohio: a five-story building had to come down without disturbing the neighboring structures. His preparation needed to be exactly right. When he pushed the plunger the whole thing crumbled in seconds and nothing else suffered.

We've all seen the fictional version of dynamite explosions with fragments of material flying into the air in all directions after an ear-splitting earth-shaking detonation. For the location of our house we chose the highest part of our property in spite of a huge boulder right in the middle. We called our neighbor, Jimmy Decker, to blast it out.

He and his helper spent six hours drilling 127 holes into the rock and carefully filling them with blasting powder connected to a wire. Ready for the detonation, we walked back about 500 yards. Jimmy pushed the plunger. There was a dull thud. The rock seemed to expand a little in the ground, but nothing flew into the air except perhaps a puff of smoke from the blasting powder and a little dust. That rock was in smaller, moveable pieces, which now grace the landscape around our house.

We weren't on the site, but heard about a special job Jimmy did at Pepperdine University. He had to remove solid rock in the bottom of the Brock House swimming pool after the windows were in. To everyone's amazement, not even a crack!

Among the many interesting movie jobs, Jimmy remembered two in particular: For *Flight 223 Is Down* he set the explosives that blew up the plane, which in the story had crashed into an apartment in Compton. For *Homebodies* Jimmy dynamited an old brick building. In that story it fell apart just after it had been leased to a group of old people.

We knew Malibu's dynamiter as a good neighbor who loved the land and took great pride in his profession. He was brought up to believe in the "work ethic" and had little patience with "slacking off" or cheating in any way, shape, or form.

Chapter 25

Malibu Incorporation

(Now We are a City)

At dinner one evening shortly after another Malibu City Council election, the younger of my guests, Dianne, asked how and why had Malibu became a city. She was surprised when I told her it actually began late in 1963 (when she was just a year old).

Another guest, Dave, remembered that in 1962, Malibu was a part of Los Angeles County and had no separate legal status. These were the major issues at the time: the California State Highway Department was seriously considering several freeway routes across and over Malibu and actually had bought property that would have been in the right-of-way; the Los Angeles Department of Water and Power and the Atomic Energy Commission had plans on their books for a nuclear reactor plant at Pacific Coast Highway and Corral Canyon; Los Angeles County's assessments on real property were increasing at an alarming rate; and the deed restrictions imposed when the Marblehead Land Company sold the land were about to expire, allowing for more intensive development.

At that time, the Los Angeles County Board of Supervisors governed Malibu. A group of us, headed by my husband, decided it was time for the people of Malibu to have a legal means of determining our own destiny. We began to try and form the City of Malibu.

We circulated petitions and got the necessary number of signatures. We commissioned two study reports. One guessed there would be a high tax rate for a new city. The other showed there would be no increase in taxes for the same services provided by the county.

Malibu polarized.

The Malibu Chamber of Commerce, a local newspaper, and the majority of the Realty Board opposed the effort, maintaining taxes in a new city would be too high. The Malibu Township Council and a host of private citizens supported incorporation as the best way for Malibu.

Election Day was set for January 7, 1964. (I still remember balancing campaign duties with our holiday activities). Boundaries for the proposed city were those of Malibu Rancho from Las Flores Canyon to the Ventura County line and inland to the northerly line of the rancho. At the request of the residents, Big Rock Mesa, part of Carbon Mesa, the AEC boundaries, Trancas Canyon and Lachusa were excluded.

Thirty-seven candidates put their hats in the ring for the proposed five-seat city council. After a hard-fought campaign waged in the local and Santa Monica press, incorporation failed by 276 votes .

Nevertheless, with the threats of the freeway and the nuclear reactor hanging over our heads, Malibu's citizens managed to unite in opposition, and soundly defeated both the freeway and the reactor. The now infamous "Prop 13" passed overwhelmingly in California and eased the tax burden. That left only the deed restriction problem. With no central planning, Malibu "just growed." Another try for cityhood in 1971 couldn't get enough support and "died a-borning" without an election. A third try in 1976 was defeated by 104 votes.

Out of curiosity in 1990 I looked up those 37 original candidates. Of the 14 who remained in Malibu, nine told me they believed Malibu would have fewer land use problems had the city incorporated in 1964. Big developers had not started knocking at the door and it would have been easier for the city council to meet with them and work out an overall land development plan before the Coastal Commission came into being in 1976.

Malibu finally did become an incorporated city in 1991, with Walt Keller as the first mayor. The big issue, basically left over from 1964, remained land development, and after nearly 15 years, no overall city plan has been agreed upon. Several acrimoniously fought elections later, no agreement between growth and development is on the horizon. Neither the "city fathers," the "developers," nor the Coastal Commission can even come close to a compromise. The city council seems always to be divided between those who insist Malibu remain "rural" as it was 50 years ago (or whenever they came to live here); landowners who need to develop their property; and the Coastal Commission who visualizes Malibu as one big public park. An astonishing amount of the city's budget goes into lawsuits.

Our civic problems just do not go away. Future city councils must deal with the increasing volume of traffic on our lone highway, inadequate septic tanks, and how to deal with the problem of waste, sensible commercial development, and balancing adequate parks and playgrounds for our residents along with "public access" to our beaches.

I have to believe that some day Malibu citizens will care enough to elect a compatible city council willing and able to meet and beat all of the problems. This beautiful place deserves no less!

Chapter 26

THE SEA LION

In 1915, locked gates and armed guards at Las Flores Canyon kept motorists from going any further along the beach road from Santa Monica. Among several buildings there, was a small shack "Las Flores Inn" owned and operated by Messrs, Ed Grimshaw and Ray Golding.

In those days Las Flores Canyon was the "end of the line." It marked the eastern boundary of Rancho Topango Malibu Simi and Sequit and the gates not only were locked, but were closely guarded. Daring motorists in their touring cars could drive the narrow rocky road along the beach from Santa Monica, but all had to turn around at Las Flores.

What an ideal spot for a café, especially when the weather was fine! (But imagine the state of the unsurfaced dirt road through the Big Rock area during the winter rains). The late Judge John Webster and his wife, Nellie, had a fishing camp in Las Flores Canyon and found the Las Flores Inn a convenience, as the owners sold milk and eggs as well as meals.

Time passed. The gates to the Rancho Malibu were opened when May K. Rindge lost her law suit and the highway continued through her rancho in the 1920s. Several of my friends remembered that by the 1930's the Las Flores Inn was the stop for school buses to Santa Monica, but they said there were no sea lions there then.

When my husband and I came to live in Malibu in 1949, there were sea lions in a large chain link enclosed tank in the middle of the Las Flores Inn parking lot. On occasional Saturdays when the tide was so high our narrow beach disappeared, we'd walk up to buy seafood at the counter in the adjoining fish house and always added a couple of packages of fish heads to toss to the sea lions.

One called "Josie" was a particular pet. She barked politely but insistently when she saw a "meal" approaching. (Translate: anyone.) She would slide back and forth on the tank's edge and stand up and beg with her flippers. Little boys (and some not quite so little) would imitate her bark and all had a fine time.

Over the years everyone who traveled the highway along Malibu knew Josie, and many a restaurant meal at the Las Flores Inn was served because a family had stopped to "feed the sea lion." The tank was enlarged at least once and several more sea lions were added, but Josie remained the favorite.

In the 1955-56 Malibu directory the restaurant's name is listed as "Malibu Sea Lion (formerly Las Flores Inn)." During this time the Sea Lion was Malibu's community center for banquets, luncheons, and club dances. Malibu's music teacher, Peg Thompson, had at least one piano recital in the big banquet room.

On a winter night in 1964 the Sea Lion burned to the ground, but dauntless Chris Polos rebuilt it. Possibly it was at this time the sea lions vanished from the premises. Perhaps they perished in the fire. There seems to be no record and nobody remembers for certain.

But the restaurant remained “Sea Lion” until a new owner converted it into a “South Seas“ type place and it now is “Duke’s after the famous Hawaiian, Duke Kahonamoku.

SOURCES

Chumash

Anderson, Eugene N. Jr., The Chumash Indians of Southern California, Malki Museum Brochure No. 4, Banning, 1968

Bickford, Virginia Fay Gilmore, European Artifacts from a Chumash Cemetery (Masters Thesis Dissertation), Dept. of Anthropology, California State University, Long Beach, 1982

Bolton, Herbert Eugene, Spanish Exploration in the Southwest, 1908 (Reprint, 1963)

Brown, Alan K., Aboriginal Population in the Santa Barbara Channel, University of California Archaeological Research Facilities at Berkeley - Report of the Archaeological Survey Series, 69

Burnett, E.K., Inlaid Stone and Bone Artifacts from Southern California, New York, Museum of the American Indian, Heye Foundation, 1944

Coombs, Gary, Migration and Adaptation, Indian Missionization in California, Dissertation for PhD, Anthropology, UCLA, 1975

Curtis, Freddie – Archaeological Sites throughout Malibu

Engelhardt, Fr. Zephryn, OFM, Mission San Fernando Rey

Grant, Campbell, The Rock Paintings of the Chumash: A Study of a California Indian Culture, University of California Press, Berkeley and Los Angeles, 1966

Harrington, John Peabody, Breath of the Sun, Life in Early California As Told by a Chumash Indian, Fernando Librado to John P. Harrington (Edited with notes by Travis Hudson), Malki Museum Press, 1979

Heizer, Robert F. Handbook of North American Indians – California, Volume 8, Smithsonian Institution, 1978

-------- The Indians of California: A Critical Bibliography, 1976

------- and Albert Elsasser, The Natural World of California Indians., University of California Press, 1980

------- and A.E. Treganza Mines and Quarries of the California Indians, California Journal of Mines and Geology, July 1944

Hudson, Travis, and Ernest Underhay, Crystals in the Sky, an Intellectual Odyssey Involving Chumash Astronomy, Cosmology and Rock Art, Ballena Press, 1978

James, George Wharton, In and Out of the Old Missions of California, Boston, 1911

Krober A, L., Handbook of the Indians of America, 1926 (reprinted,1953)

Laird, Carobeth, Encounter with an Angry God, Recollections of My Life with John P. Harrington, Malki Museum Press, Morongo Indian Reservation, Banning, California, 1975

Landberg, Leif C.W., The Chumash Indians of Southern California, Southwest Museum Press, 1965

Lee, Georgia A., The Portable Cosmos: Effigies, Ornaments and Incised Stone from the Chumash area, Ballena Press Anthropological Papers, No. 21

Peck, S. L., An Archaeological Report on the Excavation of a Primitive Site at Zuma Creek, Los Angeles County, California, Archaeological Survey Association of Southern California Paper #2, Los Angeles

Phillips , George H, The Enduring Struggle — Indians in California. History, Golden State Series, San Francisco, 1981

Priestly, H. I. Ed., A Historical, Political and Natural Description Of California, by Pedro Fages, Soldier of Spain, 1937 University of California Press

Reid, Hugo, Letters of 1852 (Robert F. Heizer, Annotator and Editor), Southwest Museum Paper #21

Robinson, Alfred, Life in California, June 1, 1969 Edition, Da Capo Press

Schumacher, Paul, Ancient Graves and Shell Heaps of California, Annual Report, Regents of the Smithsonian Institution, 1860-74 Washington, pp. 335-50

UCLA, Archaeological Survey Annual Report 7 (1965), Chumash pp.1-302, Archaeology and Surviving Chumash

Underhill, Ruth, Indians of Southern California Branch of Education, Indian Affairs, U.S. Dept. of Interior – Stewart Udall

Walsh, Jane MacLean, John Peabody Harrington: The Man and His California Field Notes, Ballena Press Anthropological Papers #6, 1976

Woodward, A., Shell Fishhooks of the Chumash, 1929 Bulletin of the Southern California Academy of Science 28:41- 46, Los Angeles

------------ Indian Foodstuffs of Los Angeles County, 1949 Los Angeles County Museum. Museum Leaflet Series, History No. 1, L.A.

Tapia

Archives of Prefecture, Book A, Part II, pp. 441-443, The Will of Jose Bartolomeo Tapia, English translation with index in the vaults of the Los Angeles County Recorder

Bancroft, Hubert Howe, History of California, Volume I, 1542-1800 San Francisco, A. L. Bancroft & Company, Publishers, 1884

Baptismal Register of Mission Santa Clara (for Santiago Tapia's second family with Maria Cardenas)

Bolton, Herbert Eugene, Anza's California Expeditions – Vols. 1-4 University of California Press, Berkeley, California, 1930

Geiger, Maynard, OFM, Mission Santa Barbara

Moorhead, Max L., The Presidio—Bastion of the Spanish Borderland, University of Oklahoma Press, 1975

Northrop, Marie, Spanish American Families of Early California1769-1850, Vol II, So. Calif. Geneaological Society, Burbank, California

Pourade, Richard F., History of San Diego, "Time of the Bells," San Diego Union-Tribune Publishing Co., 1961

Sanchez, Nellie Van de Grift, Spanish Arcadia, 1929

Early Malibu

Rindge, Frederick Hastings, Happy Days in Southern California, 1898 (rededication by Rindge grandchildren, 1972)

Smith, Horace J., The Malibu Ranch, Thesis, 1944